The Story of the 2024 Tour de France

The Happy Warrior Triumphs

By Bill & Carol McGann
With contributions from David and Aaron Stanley

McGann
Publishing

Published by McGann Publishing
P.O. Box 864
McMinnville, OR 97128
USA

www.mcgannpublishing.com
ISBN 978-1-7367494-2-5

Table of Contents

Preface

This telling of the 2024 Tour de France is an addition to our two-volume The Story of the Tour de France: How a Newspaper Promotion Became the Greatest Sporting Event in the World, and four supplements:

2019: A Year of New Faces

2020: The Tour During Covid-19: Better Late Than Never

2021: The Little Cannibal Dominates

2022: The Fastest Tour Ever

2023: The Viking Again Conquers the Tour

The two-volume set is available in print, Kindle eBooks and ACX Audiobooks, and the supplements are available both as Kindle eBooks and ACX Audiobooks.

Volume One of our story told of the Tour's origins and of each edition of the race from 1903 through 1975. That last year, Bernard Thévenet was able to conquer the Belgian Lion, Eddy Merckx, and hold the man who had won more races than any other rider in cycling history to five Tour wins.

Volume Two picked up the race in 1976 with super-climber Lucien van Impe's victory and took it through 2018 and Welshman Geraint Thomas' 111-second win over Tom Dumoulin.

Except for the two world wars, the Tour has been run annually since the first edition of the race in 1903.

Note: The rider with the lowest accumulated elapsed time, which is how the Tour standings are calculated, is called the leader of the General Classification. We will generally call that time standing the "GC".

Introduction

2019 had a surprise winner in twenty-two-year-old Egan Bernal, the youngest rider to wear the race-leader's Yellow Jersey in Paris since that jersey was first awarded in 1919 and the third-youngest rider ever to have won the Tour de France.

2020 was no less surprising. After stage nineteen Slovenian racer Tadej Pogačar was sitting in second place, just 57 seconds behind fellow Slovenian and race leader Primož Roglič. Then in the Tour's penultimate stage, a 36.2-kilometer individual time trial, Pogačar delivered a stunning ride, winning the stage and beating Roglič by 1 minute, 56 seconds. That superb effort made Pogačar the winner of the 2020 Tour de France. He became the first rider to win the Tour de France on his first attempt since Laurent Fignon in 1983. He did more than win the General Classification. He also won the Mountains Classification and was the Best Young Rider. Of the four individual prizes the Tour puts up for grabs, Pogačar won three of them. And at twenty-one years old, he is also the second-youngest rider to win the Tour; twenty-year-old Henri Cornet, who won the race's second edition in 1904, remains the youngest.

The 2021 Tour had to be both re-routed and re-scheduled. The organizers had originally planned to start on July 2 in Copenhagen, Denmark, with three Danish stages before a transfer to France. But the summer's crowded sports calendar forced Tour owner ASO to change both the dates of the race and the route. To make room for the re-scheduled Tokyo Olympic Games and the Euro 2020 football championships, the revised plan was for a June 26 start in Brest, Brittany with the finale in Paris to be run on July 18. The Danish start was re-scheduled to be part of the 2022 Tour route.

Pogačar was just as dominating in the 2021 race as he had been in 2020. He had already demonstrated his incredible form by winning the single-day classic Liège–Bastogne–Liège in April. After winning the Tour's stage five individual time trial, he was effectively the leader of the Tour, being just 8 seconds behind Dutchman Mathieu van der Poel, a superb classics rider who would be dispatched once the race hit the high mountains.

And that's just what happened in stage eight, with its five categorized climbs, three of which were rated first category. Pogačar was in Yellow with a 1 minute, 48 second lead over Dutchman Wout van Aert.

Pogačar's way was made easier by his major rival Primož Roglič's crash in stage three that cost Roglič a minute. Against a racer of Pogačar's class, a minute was nearly unrecoverable. Pogačar cemented his lead by winning the two mountaintop finishes, stages seventeen and eighteen. He finished the 2021 Tour with a 5 minute, 21 second lead over Team Jumbo-Visma's Jonas Vingegaard. And again, he won both the Mountains and Young Rider classifications as he had in 2020. It was a stunning performance.

The 2022 Tour de France did get its Danish start, the first stage being a 13.2-kilometer individual time trial in Copenhagen. It wasn't an easy beginning to the race, with rain falling during the afternoon start. Worse, the course wound its way around the Danish capital through twenty-three curves and corners. Indicative of the danger Stefan Bissegger, the eighth rider off, slipped and fell on one of the curves.

Despite the conditions, the favorites all finished within a half-minute of the winner, Belgian time trial champion Yves Lampaert. Pogačar followed in at 7 seconds, Jonas Vingegaard at 15, Roglič at 16 and Geraint Thomas at 25 seconds.

It was stage five, 157 kilometers with eleven cobbled sectors that profoundly changed the 2022 Tour's trajectory. As has been said for many decades, a rider won't win the Tour de France on a stage like this, but he could surely lose it. With less than forty kilometers to go, Roglič crashed, brought down by a stray hay bale. Incredibly, he put his now-dislocated shoulder back in place with his own hands and then set off with help from teammates. He finished the stage about two minutes after Tadej Pogačar. The next day Pogačar took the GC lead with American rider Neilson Powless second and Roglič teammate Jonas Vingegaard third, just 31 seconds back.

Roglič gamely stayed in the Tour. But it was too much for the injured rider who by stage fourteen was in 21st place, down 33 minutes, 39 seconds on GC leader Jonas Vingegaard. He did not start stage fifteen, deciding with his team that he needed to let his injuries heal. For the second year in a row Roglič did not finish the Tour.

But Pogačar ran out of gas before he ran out of Tour. Stage eleven was a monster climbing stage. Vingegaard attacked on the final ascent, the Col du Granon, and finished alone, a minute ahead of his nearest chaser Nairo Quintana, and almost three minutes ahead of Pogačar. The Dane now led Pogačar by 2 minutes, 16 seconds. In stage eighteen with its hilltop finish at Hautacam, Vingegaard cemented his GC lead by finishing a minute ahead of Pogačar. That gave him a 3 minute, 26 second lead, which he grew by another 8 seconds in the last time trial.

Vingegaard rode the final stage in Paris conservatively—wanting to stay safe in the Tour's final kilometers he let Pogačar grab 50 seconds— but the Tour was the Dane's. He had ridden a near-perfect Tour guarded by a powerful and capable Jumbo-Visma team.

The 2023 Tour started in Spain's Basque Country, the Tour's 25th foreign start. The race would spend three stages on the western side of the Pyrenees with the rest of the Tour being run in France. This edition would visit all five of France's mountain ranges. The riders would climb in this order, the Pyrenees, the Massif Central, the Jura, the Alps and the Vosges. To make things even more interesting, in stage nine, the riders would ascend Puy de Dôme for the first time since 1988. To win this Tour a rider would need wings.

As expected, the race started out as a duel between Vingegaard and Pogačar. By the end of the mountainous sixth stage Vingegaard was in yellow with Pogačar just 25 seconds back. Pogačar won stage six with its ascents of the Col d'Aspin, Col du Tourmalet and a first-category, 16-kilometer Cauterets-Cambasque climb to finish the stage. He crossed the finish line with a deep bow, 24 seconds ahead of Vingegaard. Vingegaard's lead over Pogačar was cut about in half, to 25 seconds.

That's the way it stayed until the deeply anticipated ninth stage with its trip up Puy de Dôme, a lava dome that is a climb of 13 kilometers averaging 7.7 percent. It wasn't unusual in that a small group escaped and stayed away. Michael Woods of the Israel-Premier Tech team crossed the finish line alone, 28 seconds ahead of his nearest chaser, Pierre Latour. But the real action was more than eight minutes back. With four kilometers to go up the dead volcano there were eight superb riders in the Yellow Jersey group: Jonas Vingegaard and Sepp Kuss

(Jumbo-Visma), Tadej Pogačar and Adam Yates (UAE Team Emirates), Carlos Rodríguez and Tom Pidcock (INEOS Grenadiers), Jai Hindley (Bora-hansgrohe), and Simon Yates (Jayco-AlUla). With just 1.5 kilometers to go Pogačar attacked. Vingegaard reacted, but the white jersey'd Pogačar was gone. He finished 600 meters ahead of Vingegaard, meaning a net gain of eight seconds. The GC gap was down to 17 seconds.

Nothing changed over the next few days until the thirteenth stage, 137.8-kilometers that weren't terribly challenging until the final 17 kilometers, an ascent of the *hors catégorie* Grand Colombier. Pogačar attacked with a bit more than 400 meters to go and gained 4 seconds on the Dutchman plus another 4 seconds in time bonus for being third in the stage. Now the time gap was just 9 seconds.

Pogačar might have been showing the first signs of fatigue in the stage sixteen timed hill-climb. Vingegaard was masterful, being the fastest at each time check. Not bothering to change from a specialist time-trial bike for a hill-climbing bike, Vingegaard was a huge 1 minute, 38 seconds faster than Pogačar, who did change bikes for the climb to the finish. Vingegaard now led by 1 minute, 48 seconds.

Stage seventeen with a hilltop finish at Courcheval settled things. Just 15 kilometers into the stage Pogačar crashed while going at a moderate speed on an uphill section after touching wheels with another rider. He was soon up and returned to riding with Vingegaard. Did he suffer real damage in the crash? Impossible to say. But on the final ascent, 16 kilometers from the finish, Pogačar was dropped from the Yellow Jersey group. While watching Vingegaard ride away up the mountain, Pogačar said into the team race radio, "I'm gone, I'm dead."

The Reuters News Agency later quoted him as saying, "I came to the foot of the climb totally empty. I ate a lot but it didn't come to my legs. I'm extremely disappointed. It was one of the worst days on a bike in my life."

He finished 5 minutes, 45 seconds behind Vingegaard. Whatever the reason was for Pogačar's *défaillance*, winning this Tour was now out of reach for him. He was now 7 minutes, 35 seconds behind race leader Vingegaard.

Pogačar found a bit of redemption when he won the twentieth stage, but Vingegaard finished at the same time. The time bonus reduced Vingegaard's lead slightly, to 7 minutes, 29 seconds.

The Story of the 2024 Tour de France

And that's how the 2023 Tour ended. Vingegaard had won his second consecutive Tour as Pogačar had done in 2020 and 2021. The 2024 Tour would probably break the tie.

So please join us for the 2024 Tour as we go on the 111th trip around La Belle France.

Chapter 1
The 2024 Racing Season So Far

The 2024 road season got its traditional start in Australia with the Tour Down Under, run January 16–21. Generally the Grand Tour GC competitors hold off racing this early, but there were some Tour dark horses making their presence known. Stephen Williams (Israel-Premier Tech) won the race with Jhonatan Narvaez (INEOS Grenadiers) a close second.

The other popular Southern Hemisphere season starter, Argentina's Vuelta a San Juan, was not on the UCI calendar for 2024.

For the riders looking for an early Euro start to their season, the Vuelta Ciclista a Mallorca was perfect, five individual races on the Mediterranean island in late January. Brandon McNulty, Aleksandr Vlasov and Rui Costa showed good form.

Grand Tour GC competitors generally wait until a bit later in the season before starting to race. Two March week-long stage races, Paris–Nice in France and Tirreno–Adriatico in Italy are popular with Grand Tour riders.

Over in Italy, Jonas Vingegaard triumphed in the Tirreno–Adriatico, with Juan Ayuso, Jai Hindley, Ben O'Connor and Tom Pidcock also in the top ten.

Paris–Nice's final GC showed the cream rising to the top. In the final top ten were winner and American *wunderkind* Matteo Jorgenson, plus Remco Evenepoel, Brandon McNulty, Mattias Skjelmose, Aleksandr Vlasov, Egan Bernal and Primož Roglič.

In a single moment in early April, the season's outlook was turned upside down. In the fourth stage of Spain's Tour of the Basque Country (*Vuelta al País Vasco*), just 35 kilometers from the finish, there was a terrible crash. Among the fallen were Jonas Vingegaard, Remco

Evenepoel and Primož Roglič. Vingegaard was taken away in an ambulance.

The crash was particularly cruel to Vingegaard. He suffered a broken collarbone and several ribs as well as a collapsed lung. Evenepoel was diagnosed with a broken collarbone and scapula. Though he suffered no broken bones, Roglič was bruised enough to abandon as well.

Roglič raced no more that spring but was on the Tour's start list as a member of his Bora-hansgrohe team, along with Jai Hindley and Aleksandr Vlasov.

Switzerland's Tour de Romandie is a week-long stage race that has long been popular with Tour aspirants. Carlos Rodriguez, Team INEOS Grenadiers' pick to lead the hunt for a Tour win, beat Aleksandr Vlasov by just 7 seconds for the final race win.

On May 4 the Giro d'Italia started near Torino. In that starting peloton were a few riders with serious Tour hopes. Among the GC riders planning on doing the Giro–Tour double were Geraint Thomas, Tadej Pogačar, and Romain Bardet.

Pogačar delivered a stunning Giro ride. In stage two with its hilltop finish, Pogačar showed that he had not come to play. He soloed across the finish line nearly a half-minute ahead of ten chasers, having dropped such fine riders as Daniel Martinez and Geraint Thomas.

Come the 2024 Giro's first time trial, 40 kilometers with an uphill finish, Pogačar again displayed his superiority, beating five-time Italian and two-time world time trial champion Filippo Ganna by 17 seconds. He now led the Giro by 2 minutes, 17 seconds.

Ganna got revenge in the stage fourteen time trial, beating Pogačar by 29 seconds over 31.2 kilometers. Despite Ganna's winning the stage, that second place extended Pogačar's lead to 3 minutes, 41 seconds over now-second-place Geraint Thomas.

Come the high Alps he won two stages in a row and then in stage seventeen had to settle for just second place. Over those three days Pogačar grew his lead to 7 minutes, 42 seconds.

Pogačar wasn't weakening. Over the mountains of the Giro's penultimate stage Pogačar left everyone 2 minutes, 7 seconds back.

The final tally after the finish in Rome: Pogačar had won the 2024 Giro d'Italia by 9 minutes, 56 seconds over Daniel Martinez. Geraint Thomas was third, another 30 seconds back.

And now he was going to try for the Giro–Tour double, last done in 1998 by a surely-drugged Marco Pantani.

There were two more pre-Tour week-long races. The Critérium du Dauphiné is not only a last chance to tune the legs before the Tour, on its own it is a prestigious race that has been run since 1947. It is also the only race that has been won by all four of the five-time Tour winners. Primož Roglič won the 2024 edition by just 8 seconds over American racer Matteo Jorgenson. Roglič came very close to not winning: he almost ran out of gas before he ran out of race. Going into the final stage he had a 62-second lead over Jorgenson. The Dauphiné's final climb was the 9.4 kilometer Col de Glières, which rears up to the skies with a 7.1 percent gradient. On that ascent Roglič faltered, finishing 48 seconds behind Jorgenson. That was just enough, leaving Roglič with those precious 8 seconds of lead.

The other pre-Tour race is the Tour of Switzerland, run June 9–June 16 in 2024. The race was almost the private property of UAE Team Emirates rider Adam Yates. Yates won the GC by 22 seconds over teammate Joao Almeida. He also won the points and mountains classifications. Despite that dominating ride, he would be riding the Tour in service of his team leader Tadej Pogačar.

Chapter 2
The 2024 Tour de France Route

On October 25, 2023 Christian Prudhomme, director-general of the Tour de France since 2007, announced the route of the 2024 Tour de France at the usual venue, Paris' Palais des Congrès. This Tour would not end in Paris, finishing instead in Nice. With the 2024 Summer Olympic Games being held July 26–August 11 in Paris, the final stage would be run on the French Riviera to avoid a logistical and security nightmare. In fact, the farthest north this Tour would get would be the ancient city of Troyes, about 140 kilometers southeast of Paris.

Again, Prudhomme broke with tradition. For the first time the Tour would start in Italy, Florence to be exact, on Saturday, June 29. There would be no riding into form during this Tour's early stages. From Florence in Tuscany the riders would head east to Rimini on the Adriatic coast and encounter seven climbs.

It wouldn't get any easier in stage two. The riders were pointed back west to Bologna with six climbs in the way.

Finally, the sprinters would get a day as the Tour headed west, south of Milan for a finish in Turin. There was nothing in the three rated climbs that should keep a world-class sprinter from making it to the front of the pack to fight for a stage win.

Stage four would take the riders out of Italy and into France, but not without going into the thin air of the high Alps. The riders would have to go over the Sestrière and Montgenèvre climbs before encountering the monstrous Col du Galibier, 23 kilometers averaging 5.1 percent. This would be the sixty-fourth time the Tour had sent riders over that mountain since it was first used in the 1911 edition of the Tour. The Galibier was made the *Souvenir Henri Desgrange*, meaning the first rider to the top of the peak would get an award and a cash prize. This again makes clear that riders contending for the GC would have to come to this Tour ready to race. The organizers wrote, "A difficult excursion to 2,642 meters above sea level on day four of the race: the peloton has never climbed so high so early." There was a time when Tour GC contenders would come at less than peak form and spend the first ten days of racing getting to top form. Those days would seem to be gone.

The sprinters would finally have a little more raw meat to chew on with stages five and six being flat. Their romp across eastern France would be interrupted by stage seven's 25-kilometer individual time trial finishing in Gevrey-Chambertin in eastern France. The race was now just south of Dijon in serious winemaking country, on the *Route des Grands Crus*.

The sprinters would get another bite of the apple in stage eight before the brutal ninth stage and its 32 kilometers of gravel roads, the Tour's version of Italy's Strade Bianche race. Richard Plugge, CEO of Vingegaard's Jumbo-Visma team said, "I think it is a bit unnecessary. It increases the chance of bad luck. We want the fight to be as fair as possible. A ride like this, in my opinion, does not contribute to that."

Vingegaard was also clearly less than tickled by a day on gravel, "It will be a new experience as it will be the first time I ride on gravel during a race. It's a day where you can lose more than you can gain. We will have to make do with the choice of the course builders."

After the day on the graveled roads the riders would have their first rest day and a short transfer to Orléans for stage ten's 187-kilometer trip almost due south to the small town of Saint-Amand-Montrond, Julian Alaphilippe's home town.

Back into the hills, the Massif Central to be specific, for stage eleven's finish at the ski town of Le Lioran. Then two flat stages taking the race to the Pyrenees. On Saturday July 13, stage fourteen's trip to Saint-Lary-Soulan/Plat d'Adet would send the riders over the Tourmalet and the Hourquette d'Ancizan before the 10.6-kilometer climb to Saint-Lary-Soulan. The Tour has sent riders up the 8.2 kilometer, 5.1 percent climb regularly, this being the eleventh time since 1974.

Sunday's stage fifteen was no easier with the legendary climbs Col de Peyresourde, Col de Menté, the Col d'Agnes and a finish atop Plateau de Beille, 15.8 kilometers averaging 7.9 percent.

Finally, the second rest day with a short eastward transfer to Gruissan for the final week in the Alps. The stage from Gruissan to Nîmes would be a flat prelude to the upcoming climbing. That climbing would come in Wednesday's stage seventeen, with a 178-kilometer trip to the Alpine ski resort of Superdévoluy. The stage would first send the riders up the Col Bayard (first used in the Tour in 1905) and the Col du Noyer before the 3.8-kilometer, 5.9-percent road to the ski resort, the first time the Tour has used Superdévoluy for a stage finish.

Friday, July 19, the Tour's nineteenth stage would again send the riders up to nosebleed heights. In just 145 kilometers, the riders would first confront the Col de Vars and the Cime de la Bonette before a finish at another ski resort, Isola 2000 at the end of a 16.1 kilometer, 7.1 percent road.

This Tour would not relent. The 2024 Tour's penultimate stage, number twenty, started in Nice and headed into the Alpes Maritimes culminating in a finish atop the Col de la Couillole.

One might think that going into the final stage, a 35-kilometer time trial starting in Monaco and finishing in Nice, that the hard climbing might been completed. Nope. The chrono sent the riders over two climbs, the 8.1 kilometer La Turbie, averaging a 5.6 percent gradient and then the Col d'Eze, just a 1.6 kilometer climb, but with a tough 8.1 percent gradient.

The owner of the Yellow Jersey has not changed hands on the final day since Greg LeMond's eight-second win over Laurent Fignon in 1989. Might it happen in 2024?

Chapter 3
Teams and Riders

We will start with the GC contenders:

Tadej Pogačar (UAE Team Emirates): The 2020 and 2021 Tour winner (second places in 2022 and 2023) had a stunning spring. For starters, he won both the Giro d'Italia's GC and mountains classifications, earning six stage wins along the way. But as the infomercial announcer says, "But wait! There's more!" He won two of the most important single-day races on the calendar, Liège–Bastogne–Liège and Strade Bianche. He was third in Milano–Sanremo.

In Spain he was merciless to the competition. He made the March week-long Volta a Catalunya his own, winning the GC, points and mountains classifications, and four of the seven stages. In the final stage he made his extraordinary form clear. Despite the stage's six second-category and one third-category climbs, twenty-three riders were still together for the sprint. Pogačar, wearing the race leader's jersey, won the sprint.

And now this man wanted to do what no racer had done in a generation, win the Giro and Tour the same season. If he succeeded, he would be joining a club of immortals. Only seven riders have accomplished the difficult double: Fausto Coppi (1949 & 1952), Jacques Anquetil (1964), Eddy Merckx (1970, 1972, 1974), Bernard Hinault (1982, 1985), Stephen Roche (1987), Miguel Indurain (1992, 1993) and Marco Pantani (1998). It has so far been done twelve times.

But at a Pre-Tour news conference on the Thursday before the Tour start Pogačar, according to *Bicycling Magazine*, "Dropped a Bomb". He announced that after winning the Giro he had contracted Covid, "About ten days ago, I had a Covid infection. It caused some doubts, but I've recovered well. Covid isn't as serious anymore these days, especially not when you already had the virus in the past. It was over soon." He said he took one day off training, had cold-like symptoms, then did a day on the rollers before resuming he regular training program. Was he really back up to speed? There is no tougher test than the Tour de France and his condition would soon be revealed.

Jonas Vingegaard (Visma | Lease a Bike): Vingegaard won the 2022 and 2023 Tours. In 2023 he also won the Tour of the Basque Country, the Critérium du Dauphiné and Spain's O Gran Camiño. Late in the season he participated in his team's domination of the Vuelta a España. The team (then called Jumbo-Visma) won the first three places in the GC, with Vingegaard coming in second to Sepp Kuss and ahead of Primož Roglič. All in all, an incredible season and an extraordinary season-ending flourish for the team.

In 2024 Vingegaard looked to be on the same trajectory, winning O Gran Camiño in late February and Tirreno–Adriatico in early March.

We noted earlier that he broke his collarbone and several ribs in a crash in the Tour of the Basque Country's fourth stage. It looked to this writer that his bid for a third Tour win would have to wait a year. His sports director Merijn Zeeman said, "Jonas only goes to the Tour if he is one hundred percent."

On June 20 the team announced that Vingegaard would ride the Tour with this post: "The Danish two-time Tour winner has recovered enough from his crash in the Tour of the Basque Country to fight for a good result.

Vingegaard worked hard over those two months to get fit in time. "I am excited to start the Tour. The last few months have not always been easy, but I thank my family and Team Visma | Lease a Bike for their unwavering support. We have worked together to get to this moment, and of course, I am very excited to see where I stand. I feel good and very motivated."

Zeeman added, "I am very proud of Jonas and the coaching team. He is coming back from a serious injury. In the last few weeks, he has shown what a champion he is, both mentally and physically. Of course, we don't know how far he can go yet. We are being cautious because he has not been able to race, and his preparation has been less than ideal, to say the least. But he will be there, healthy and motivated."

Primož Roglič (Bora-hansgrohe): Chris Froome wrote this about the Vuelta a España and Giro d'Italia winner: "He's one of the most cunning and crafty riders I've ever raced against and he's got incredible resilience, which is such an important factor when it comes to competing for the top three steps in a Grand Tour. He won the recent edition of the Critérium du Dauphiné, and while I know he showed a little bit of weakness on that final stage, I still think that he's going to find another level at the Tour de France." He had also crashed in the Tour of the Basque Country, but suffered only minor injuries, from which he had recovered.

Remco Evenepoel (Soudal Quick-Step): Evenepoel looks like the sport's most naturally talented racer since Greg LeMond. He spent most of his youth playing soccer, but thinking that his athletic talents were better suited to bicycle racing, switched to the two-wheeled sport in 2017. The next year he won both the time trial and road race at both the European Junior Road Cycling Championships and the Junior World Championships. He's been on an upward arc ever since.

Evenepoel turned pro in 2019 and in June won the Tour of Belgium GC and points classification as well as a stage. He proved his single-day racing chops by winning the World Tour Clásica de San Sebastián in August of that same year. He crowned his first pro road season with a silver medal at the World Time Trial Championships.

The next year, four prestigious week-long stage races were his. In 2021, his momentum slowed a bit but in 2022 he had a stunning year. He won his first grand Tour, the Vuelta a España, The Tour of Norway, the Volta ao Algarve and two single-day classics, Liège–Bastogne–Liège and the Clásica de San Sebastián. Plus, he won the World Road Championships. He would spend 2023 wearing a rainbow jersey.

He achieved many high-value race wins in 2023, both single-day and stage races, including the UAE Tour, repeats of Liège–Bastogne–Liège and the Clásica de San Sebastián wins. He was leading the Giro d'Italia when he tested positive for Covid-19 and had to abandon.

In August he won the World Time Trial Championships. This extraordinarily talented Belgian had all the ability needed to win the Tour de France.

Joao Almeida (UAE Team Emirates): If Pogačar should falter, his teammate Portuguese racer Joao Almeida should be able to take on the responsibilities of team leader. He won the Tours of Poland and Luxembourg in 2021 and in 2023 was the Giro d'Italia's Best Young Rider. In 2024 he won two stages in the Tour de Suisse and finished second, 22 seconds behind teammate Adam Yates.

Adam Yates (UAE Team Emirates): UAE Team Emirates has incredible depth. Adam Yates, now 31, won the Tour's Young Rider classification in 2016. Since then he's been first in the Tour de Romandie, Tour de Suisse, Volta a Catalunya, the UAE Tour and other prestigious races. In 2016 he was fourth in the Tour and in 2023 was third. He also has a fourth place in the 2021 Vuelta a España. Importantly, his Tour de Suisse win came in 2024. He's tanned, fit and ready to race the Tour.

Romain Bardet (Team dsm-firmenich PostNL): Every year I hope Romain Bardet will break on through to the other side. He has come so close, second in the Tour in 2016, third in 2017. Might he put everything together for a successful run to win the Yellow Jersey or has time passed the thirty-three-year-old racer by?

And who might end up with the Green Jersey of the Tour's best sprinter? This year's Tour has a bumper crop of fast-twitch men to fight for the sprint wins.

Mark Cavendish (Astana Qazaqstan): Surely Cavendish is the sentimental favorite of all the sprinters. Going onto the 2024 Tour, The Manx Missile had thirty-four stage wins, the same as all-time racing great Eddy Merckx. He had considered retiring at the end of the 2023 season but decided to continue racing in the hope that he could win another stage and be the outright owner of the Tour stage win record. Could the thirty-nine-year old sprinter who had been racing professionally since 2005 win a stage in the world most important race?

Jasper Philipsen (Alpecin-Deceuninck): Philipsen was the winner of the points classification in 2023, taking four stages along the way. His 2024 season started splendidly with a win in Milano–Sanremo and a second in Paris–Roubaix. Philipsen has an explosive jump as well as a lot of endurance that sees him competitive at the end of long races that don't have too much climbing.

Biniam Girmay (Intermarché-Wanty): In 2022 Biniam Girmay became the first black African cyclist to win a Grand Tour stage when he won stage ten of the Giro d'Italia. That year he also won the single-day classic Gent–Wevelgem. The next year he got a couple of wins and in the 2024 season he took Australia's Surf Coast Classic and in Europe the Circuit Franco-Belge. A second in Rund um Köln to Dutchman Casper van Uden seemed to speak of a lot of potential that was yet unrealized.

Arnaud De Lie (Lotto Dstny): Young and truly talented, the 22-year-old sprinter won nine pro races in 2022 and eight in 2023. And they were not unimportant races. His 2023 wins included the GP Cycliste de Quebec, GP du Morbihan, the Polynormande as well the final points classification in the Etoile de Bessèges.

Jonas Abrahamsen (Uno-X Mobility): Though Abrahamsen turned pro in 2014, he had no significant wins or high placings until 2024. In early June he won one of the oldest races on the calendar, the Brussels Cycling Classic and he did it in style. He mounted a late attack and crossed the finish line 4 seconds ahead of the pack led in by Biniam Girmay.

Wout van Aert (Visma | Lease a Bike): Since making road a serious priority instead of cyclocross when he moved to the Jumbo-Visma (now Visma | Lease a Bike) team in 2019, van Aert has won more than thirty races, many of them the most prestigious and important on the calendar: Milano–Sanremo, Strade Bianche, Amstel Gold, Gent–Wevelgem, Omloop Het Nieuwsblad and ten Tour de France stages. Going into the Tour, he had just two 2024 race wins, Kuurne–Brussels–Kuurne and a stage in the Volta ao Algarve.

Wait there's more to our preview!

Regular contributor to my web site BikeRaceInfo.com and voice artist for this and many of our other books, polymath David Stanley and his son Aaron sent me a set of topics on the upcoming 2024 Tour de France to discuss, and then David and Aaron sent me their thoughts about each topic without knowing what the other has written.

1a) Who is/are the betting favorite(s)?

David: My original lede was something like "BET THIS MONTH'S MORTGAGE ON TADEJ AND THE BOYS FROM UAE!!!" I don't think that has changed. Even though Jumbo | Lease a Bike has been sandbagging like the Red River of the North in North Dakota when it's about to crest over the top of its banks, even an 80% Jonas Vingegaard and Wout van Aert can shake things up. That is the big question, isn't it? How race-fit, without any race days and following horrific crashes, can Vingegaard and van Aert possibly be?

In a prior era, it was impossible to get race-fit without race days. It was just impossible to be that fine-tuned. But in 2024, our ability to track and influence fitness has tossed most of our training truisms right out the window. In addition, the official word from Jumbo | Lease a

Bike is that just being in the mix is enough, where earlier the word was that Vingegaard wouldn't race unless he was capable of the win. I think Jumbo | Lease a Bike is not exactly being forthright. I expect them to be ready to race.

It doesn't matter. The UAE Emirates Express is loaded for bear. Adam Yates, Joao Almeida, and Juan Ayuso could all lead Grand Tour teams and win. While Sepp Kuss and Matteo Jorgenson and Wout van Aert are proven, stellar teammates, you still have to like the UAE boys. On the flats, it's no contest. Tim Wellens and Nils Pollitt are beasts, pure and simple. We've not seen a squad like this since the days of the Sky Express, The Postal Blue Train, and Eddy's Men in Orange. Feel free to bet a reasonable amount of your monthly budget on the UAE squad.

(I hear you from here—"What about Primož Roglič and Geraint Thomas?" Those two are exceptional racers, with outstanding palmares, full respect to both. I put them, at this stage of their careers, at the same level as Matteo Jorgenson. Except Matteo is in the ascendancy and Primož and Geraint are on the other side of the slope. They should finish in the Top Ten, but a podium? I don't see it.)

A Bike Race Haiku:
> This year's Tour de France
> Promises much excitement.
> My winner? Tadej.

Aaron: You, me, and the bookies would all be remiss in saying any name other than Tadej Pogačar here. He's on a run of form rarely seen in any sport. He has a loaded roster around him, and he has the aura of a man competing with the sort of *joie de vivre* that only comes with knowing you're a generational talent having the time of their life doing the thing they love the most. If offered Pog vs The Field, I'd be taking Pog.

1b) Who is/are the sentimental favorite(s)?

David: I have two choices in the sentimental favorites category. One is EF-EasyPost's Neilson Powless. I love his grinta and panache and sense of humor. He's got no chance of winning the *maillot jaune*, but the polka dots remain a very strong possibility for him and for sure, he'll be in my Velogames Fantasy team. My other sentimental favorite is Tom Pidcock from INEOS. I am in awe at the way Pidders can swap back and forth between cycling disciplines and not lose a bike length to anyone, especially on the true alpine puckering descents. I do believe he has a reasonable chance to grab a podium spot, and again, he'll be in my squad. The kid is a huge talent, and will only be improving over the next few years.

Aaron: Thibaut Pin- oh, sorry, it's 2024 now. Romain Bardet, then. The tortured poets' society that is French Grand Tour contenders will soon add another member to its illustrious list of alumni, as he announced that 2024 will be his final Tour de France and the 2025 Dauphiné will be his final road race. Can he win the Tour? Almost certainly not. Can he go out in a blaze of glory, seeking combative prizes and breakaways every chance he gets? That much, I think, sounds doable for the lovable racer who always came up just short of reaching the top step of the podium on the Champs-Elysées.

2a) Which young guy is likely to have a break-out Tour?

David: This is Ben Healy's time. He's twenty-three, had an outstanding year in 2023, and I see him getting into an early break on either the punchy stage two or the truly mountainous fourth stage, and if he takes a fair amount of time, he might claim the *maillot jaune* for several days, perhaps even a week, as Steve Bauer did in 1990 in similar circumstances when he wore Yellow for nine days.

Aaron: Derek Gee will be making his Tour de France debut after finishing twenty-second last year at the Giro (in his first-ever Grand Tour, no less) and third at the Dauphiné a few weeks ago, complete with a stage win and a day in the Yellow Jersey. He'll be at the reins of an Israel-Premier Tech squad not short on experience. And with the kind of momentum he's built up, the sky's the limit—though it remains to be seen whether or not he'll be given a bit of a leash by the true GC favorites if he tries to contest stage victories.

My honorable mention goes to Juan Ayuso, who'll play an important role for UAE in the mountains and who already has two top-five finishes at the Vuelta under his belt. Oh, and did I mention his win at the Tour of the Basque Country, second place at Tirreno-Adriatico, and fifth at the Tour de Romandie this season? Oh yeah, and he's only 21 years old.

2b) Which American is likely to star? Can he podium?

David: I have to go with Matteo Jorgenson (Visma | Lease a Bike) as the top US rider. He had an incredible spring, comes into the Tour de France well-rested, and he is ready to prove that he can ride with the very best on the World's Biggest Stage. If Jonas falters, look for Visma to turn to Matteo, with his mix of solid time trial riding and faultless climbing. Can he podium? It would be unlikely. Is MJ of that quality? Just about. Is he ready to seize that moment? I hope so.

Aaron: Matteo Jorgenson may be in the best form of any rider on a roster that includes Jonas Vingegaard, Wout van Aert, Christophe Laporte, and Sepp Kuss. While he comes into the Tour ostensibly riding in support of Vingegaard, his win at Paris–Nice and second-place finish at the Dauphiné are proof-positive that he is ready to take the next step when it comes to competing in Grand Tours. A podium might be a tough ask this year, especially given the uncertain status of Visma's strategy for this Tour, but a top ten would be a great—and achievable—result.

2c) Favorite flatlands domestique?

David: Nils Pollitt. End of story. A few months back, I was watching the 2023 Tour de France highlights while riding the trainer. Pollitt was rolling along at 30+ miles per hour for a while. He shattered his chain riding at a constant speed. Now, I've broken chains, but always when I've been doing jumps. But to be so freaking strong that you can break a chain that is under constant pressure? That, friends, is beast-mode achieved.

Aaron: Nils Pollitt on this year's UAE squad feels like their equivalent to a left tackle in the NFL: not a flashy player like the quarterback (Pogačar) or wide receivers (Almeida, Ayuso, Yates), but quietly one of the most important positions on the field. He'll be tasked with dragging a roster full of climbing talent through the flat and rolling stages, a largely thankless job that will go unnoticed by many but a role which is key to success in the big picture. Keep an eye out for him at the head of the peloton day in and day out, putting in tireless hours to make sure Pog and Co. are kept safe and sound outside of the high mountains.

3) Cavendish and Astana: will they or won't they?

David: People forget, Cav is a damned fine bike racer, not just one of the all-time great sprinters. He can do a lot more than ride the wheels until there are 1,500 meters to go. He can get into any group and win. He's not a climber, but he can get over the climbs. He has the finest lead-out guy, Michael Morkov, as his lead-out guy (and it's always good to have a guy). Does Cav take that stage, despite now longer being one of the top speed guys? Yes, he does.

Aaron: Mark Cavendish has not achieved his CVS-receipt-long list of stage wins without some sheer grit and toughness, and knowing that this is his last Tour—and consequently his last chance to break the all-time stage wins record—will only add more fuel to his considerable competitive fire. Is he, at thirty-nine years old, as fast as the Philipsens and the Pedersens of the world? Almost assuredly not. Can he use every ounce of knowledge, strategy, bike handling, and willpower he has to find the lone stage win standing between him and the record books? I think so.

4) Remco Evenepoel: stage hunter, spoiler, or true podium contender?

David: Remco has a problem. Of the top guys, he has the weakest team. He may be twenty-four, but he rides with a very experienced head. That will serve him well as he looks to profit from the battles between INEOS, Visma | Lease a Bike, and UAE. I believe he'll win a stage or three, the time trial for sure, and he'll podium. In fact, I like him to push Jonas down to the third step. Here's my podium: Tadej, Remco, and Jonas.

Aaron: The needle has swung wildly on Evenepoel over the past year or so, to the point where it's nearly impossible to predict what's to come for him—and not through any fault of his own, following the brutal injuries he fell victim to at the Tour of the Basque Country. A podium spot, after seeing how he looked at the Dauphiné, seems a distant dream, but a stage win—perhaps at one of the two medium-distance individual time trials?—could still be an obtainable goal, with the finishing stage a juicy target should he fall out of the GC picture before the final few high mountain days.

5) Whither Froomey now?

David: It happens with too many great athletes. They don't realize that, for them, the band has stopped playing and it's time to go home. I loved watching Froomey: his ability to spin up from 85 to 110 rpm on a nine percent slope, his focus and concentration, his ability to lead the squad, his all-around talent on the bike. Seven Grand Tours. I understand, a horrible crash stole his last productive seasons, and he wants them back. Yet, even without the crash, at thirty-nine, he's past his athletic sell-by date.

It happens to athletes in every sport and the list is long. Athletes with the courage to quit near the height of powers are rare. American football's Jim Brown and Barry Sanders are among those few, and they are revered for their decision. Life in the limelight is addictive and we all want "another one." Chris, please, enough.

Aaron: Froome is thirty-nine years old, with a *palmares* that stands among the greats of all time, but the fact remains that he hasn't had a major result since 2018 and has suffered more injuries than can easily be listed here in the years since. It's clear that his best years are firmly in the rearview, and one has to wonder if it's time to move on.

6) More blue kit? Is this necessary?

David: Twenty-two teams of eight men each, yes? Twelve teams (Visma, FDJ, AG2R, Alpecin, Bora, Lidl, Movistar, Quickstep, DSM, Israel-Premier Tech, Astana and Jayco) clad in some shade of darkish blue. Ninety-six riders out of 176 in total wearing blue. Or indigo. Or cobalt. Or cornflower. Basta! Someone talk to those designers about using all of the color wheel. At least, throw in some splashes of blue's complement: a bit of orange would be lovely.

Aaron: AG2R. FDJ. Alpecin. Bora. Lidl. Movistar. Quickstep. DSM. Israel-Premier Tech. Astana. Jayco. And now, Visma. Visma-LAB was one of the few holdouts in a world full of blue uniforms, and now they, too, have bent the knee to the onslaught of navy that has beset the peloton. The beehive is no more; one of a very few team kits that actually stood out in a field awash with ocean hues replaced for this Tour by a pattern that, while unique in its own right, will fade into the obscurity of yet another blue jersey among so many others when viewed on the television screen. Gone are the days of the Mapei dancing Jello cubes, gone are the days of the bright green and yellow Phonak kit. Thank God for EF and their bright pink, at least…

7) What two stages are likely to be decisive and why?

David: Stages two & four are co-choices, and stage seven will seal the deal. Stage two, 200 km from Cesenatico to Bologna, is properly hilly. Nothing but Classics-worthy up and down, six noted climbs from start to finish. The first 60 kilometers are flat, and look for an early average speed of 50+ kilometers per hour from the moment the peloton hits the *Départ Réel* at Kilometer Zero. It's a perfect opportunity, too, for UAE to put the race in the gutter, split the peloton into echelons, and launch Tadej into an early lead.

Stage four, 140 km from Pinerolo to Valloire will see massive time gaps in the true mountains between the contenders and the rest of the field. If Jonas is fit, he'll have to show his talents here or find himself struggling for the next two weeks just to gain the podium. But the true difference maker is stage seven, the 25-kilometer flat time trial from Nuits-Saint-Georges to Gevrey-Chambertin in the excellent wine-making region of Burgundy. Simply this, if you lose more than about 45 seconds in those 15 miles, you cannot win the Tour. This should be quite the battle between Tadej, Remco (I like him for the win today), and Jonas. *Contre-la-montre, pour la victoire.*

Aaron: A ferocious final week of racing this year contains the majority of the stages that are likely to be featured, and you could hardly go wrong picking any of them, but I'm going to zig where others might zag and say that I'm very interested to see how stage four plays out first and foremost. A 140-kilometer stage featuring two category-two climbs before the mighty Galibier will be an early opportunity for UAE to put their climbers at the front and challenge Vingegaard's fitness in the hopes of putting time into him early and allowing Pogačar to gain ground on his biggest rival early.

After that, all eyes will look to stage fourteen on July 13th as what may well be the most important day of this year's Tour. Fitting the Tourmalet, Ancizan, and Pla d'Adet all in 152 kilometers will present an absolutely brutal test to start a final week full of them, and everyone who's anyone will need to be present and correct on a day that could see massive time gaps if any of the favorites don't have their best legs. Whether it's Pogačar, Vingegaard, Roglič, or any of a host of other climbing stars, stage fourteen will be one to watch out for.

8) Who is the Green Jersey favorite and why is the current shade of green so ugly?

David: It has to be Jasper Philipsen (Alpecin-Deceuninck) as the overwhelming favorite. He's tremendously fast, perhaps only Jonathan Milan (Lidl-Trek) has greater top end speed, but Milan, at this writing, is not in his Tour team. Just as important, Mathieu van der Poel, when not stage hunting, has always shown himself willing to be an ace lead-out man for his teammate Philipsen. Oh, that green? It's just a bad dream from which there is no awakening. I get that it's a Skoda color, and I love that Skoda has attached themselves and their deep pockets to the Tour, but for the love of all that looks good on TV, can we maybe do a two-tone, bright cilantro green and Skoda green vertically striped points leader jersey?

Aaron: It feels a little like Jasper Philipsen versus the world in 2024 as he looks to defend his green jersey from last year, but Mads Pedersen has a very strong Lidl-Trek roster around him to challenge the returning champion on a *parcours* that features few truly "flat" stages. And who's to say freshly minted Belgian champion twenty-two-year-old Arnaud De Lie can't make some noise in his maiden Tour de France, or that Dylan Groenewegen (with Michael Matthews as his right-hand man) can't return to glory? They'll all be vying for a jersey that, disappointingly, stands out far less than its predecessor; the darker forest green just lacks a certain *je ne sais quoi* that the old bright green held. It's sad to say, but the *maillot vert* lost its aura with the change in color.

9) Which rider would you most like to hang out with for a bevvy and dinner?

David: Cav. I gave this a lot of thought (no, really, I did) and it's Mark Cavendish. He's a grown-up. The man is thirty-nine, he's been through triumph, trauma, and near-tragedy. He's been at the absolute top of the sport. He's been at the bottom of elite-level cycling. He's been cast aside. He has family and interests outside of cycling. He's an Olympic medalist, a World's winner on road and track, simply one of the best cross-venue champions ever. He's a thoughtful guy, and he also seems to be a load of fun. It has to be Cav. Maybe take a train with a dining/beverage car around the Isle of Man. A pint of Odin's Manx Ale alongside some bangers and mash in the dining car with Cav. Yeah, that's the ticket.

Aaron: I think you could learn a lot about what it means to be a professional—and pick up some valuable perspective on life in general—from spending some time around Matej Mohoric.

Chapter 4
Week One: A Tuscan Start

The race began on Saturday, June 29, with all 176 riders who had signed up to ride the Tour on the start line. For the first time in Tour history the race had an Italian start, with stage one starting in the Tuscan city of Florence.

The 206-kilometer trip from Florence to the Adriatic coastal city of Rimini was over a tough route with the Apennines in the way. The stage included three second-category climbs and four third-category climbs. The final ascent was up and over the Côte de San Marino, in the tiny country of San Marino. The riders would be either going up or going down the whole day.

It was a hot day in Tuscany with the temperature reported to be 29°C (85°F). Some teams had ice vests for the riders to wear before the race start.

To start the stage the riders paraded through the Renaissance city of Florence and crossed the Arno River by way of the Ponte Vecchio. As the riders were heading out of Florence during the 16-kilometer neutralized portion of the stage, Soudal Quick-Step rider Jan Hirt collided with a spectator's backpack and fell, breaking three teeth. The Czech rider was not deterred and rejoined the peloton. These are tough men.

And then Tour boss Christian Prudhomme dropped the flag, signaling that the neutralized portion of the stage was done and the 2024 Tour de France was on.

With such a lumpy stage facing the riders, the assumption was that a break had a good chance of succeeding and attacks started as soon as the flag was dropped. After 17 kilometers of energetic aggression a break of seven good riders got a gap. Not having any of their team members in the break, the Norwegian Uno-X Mobility team wasn't happy. Their Jonas Abrahamsen along with Lidl-Trek's Ryan Gibbons crossed the gap while climbing the 2024 Tour's first rated ascent, the second-category Col de Valico Tre Faggi.

Break rider Ion Izagirre was first over the climb. The break had built a slightly more than five-minute lead by this point. While climbers were going off the front, sprinters were being spit out the back. Speedsters Mark Cavendish, Fabio Jakobsen and Fernando Gaviria lost contact with the peloton. Back in the peloton it was American team EF Education-EasyPost that was doing the work of chasing the break.

Cavendish suffered badly during a day that did not suit his talents. Climbing hills in the terrible heat, at one point he vomited on his bike.

EF Education-EasyPost's work at the front had an effect. Come the day's second climb, the third-category Côte des Forche, the gap had been cut to 3 minutes, 40 seconds. The climbs and the day's heat took their toll. By the day's third climb the break was down to six riders, but they had increased their lead to 4 minutes, 15 seconds because EF Education-EasyPost had stopped leading the chase.

That smoked out UAE Team Emirates, who clearly had high ambitions for this Tour. They hit the front on the second-category Côte de Barbotto, about 135 kilometers into the stage. The jump in speed on the hill had several effects. The expected one was that the gap quickly fell to 2 minutes, 45 seconds. On the other hand, powerful opportunists looking for a stage win were dropped. Mads Pedersen and Mathieu van der Poel as well as GC riders Santiago Buitrago and David Gaudu were gapped.

On the second category Côte de San Leo with about 50 kilometers to go, Team Visma | Lease a Bike took over the job of working the front. Then veteran racer Romain Bardet, in the twilight of his career, took off. He flew up the mountain, joined by his Team dsm-firmenich PostNL teammate Frank van den Broek, who had dropped out of the break to join him. The pair went by the other break riders and by the next-to-last climb, the Côte de Montemaggio, they were 1 minute, 45 seconds ahead of the much-reduced peloton.

This did not sit well with INEOS Grenadiers, Lidl-Trek and EF Education-EasyPost, who gave hard chase to the duo. By the day's final climb, the Côte de San Marino, the escapees had just 1 minute, 35 seconds.

The pair put their heads down and set to work trying to stay away over the mostly flat remaining 25 kilometers. They both went deep and worked well together to keep the chasers at bay.

With 5 kilometers to go they still had a 30-second gap. It look like they would surely be caught.

But they did it! Bardet won the stage with Frank van den Broek second. The pack, lead in by Wout van Aert and Tadej Pogačar crossed the line just 5 seconds later. That was a real bike race.

Though this was Bardet's eleventh Tour, with both a second- and a third-place final GC in his results list, this was his first time to put on the Yellow Jersey. It must have felt good. In fact we know it felt good. As Bardet and van den Broek crossed the finish line they sat up with their hands in the air. He was also the first Frenchman in Yellow since Julian Alaphilippe won the first stage of the 2021 Tour.

After the stage winner Bardet said, "It's hard to describe. I couldn't really dream to achieve something like this. I think we just raced our bikes today and went for it as a team. With the way the route was and how Frank, Oscar and the rest of the team rode today, big respect and fair play to them. We just wanted to have fun and ride our bikes like there was no tomorrow. It was a long run together in the last 40 kilometers. When I had bridged across, I could feel that Frank was super pumped to have me there too, so we just went full gas to the line after that. We communicated a lot but in the end we didn't have much to say, we knew what we needed to do and just go for it until the finish. Frank is a true gentlemen, half of this jersey belongs to him. I can honestly only say all of the compliments in the world to him. We'll enjoy this as a team, it's the perfect start to the race for us."

GC contender Tadej Pogačar, "First day was super good, I tested the legs a little bit on the climbs with quite a good pace and they were ok, even with the heat. In the end I tried to sprint also, I saw an opening and I almost beat two of the fastest guys in this race, Pedersen and van Aert, but I was not lucky in the final: chapeau to the winner! Bardet and van den Broek went with a very good pace and they deserved the victory."

Stage two started in the Adriatic resort town of Cesenatico and headed northwest in a zig-zag to the ancient city of Bologna (Bologne in French). As the riders zigged and zagged through Emilia Romagna they would be sent up and over six rated climbs, all category three except a single fourth-category ascent. The start city of Cesenatico is important to many cycling enthusiasts as the hometown and resting place of Marco Pantani. Pantani is the last rider to win both the Giro d'Italia and the Tour de France in the same year. Since Pantani's drug-fueled

1998 season no one has matched that feat. I should note that Pantani never tested positive for dope during his career, though he was expelled from the 1999 Giro d'Italia for an excessively high hematocrit, a sure sign of EPO use.

But, I digress.

The day was even hotter that stage one's 29°C (85°F). Facing not only a series of relentless climbs, the riders would suffer in a day that would reach 32°C (89°F).

All 175 stage-one finishers were on the start line to contest the race to Bologna. The weather was not the only thing that was hot. Despite the pack's high-speed start, just 8 kilometers into the stage, an 11-man break managed to form. Bardet's Team dsm-firmenich PostNL didn't think any of the escapees posed a threat to Bardet's lead, so the fugitives were allowed to grow their gap. By about kilometer 66 the escapees had a lead of 8 minutes, 20 seconds.

Team Uno-X Mobility's Jonas Abrahamsen was first rider in the escape over the first two climbs. The pack wasn't comfortable with the break having such a large lead and by the top of the second climb, the Côte de Gallisterna, the gap had been brought down to 5 minutes, 35 seconds.

In the small town of Dozza where there was an intermediate sprint 108 kilometers into the stage, Wout van Aert, Matteo Jorgenson and Laurens de Plus crashed. Though scuffed up, the trio were able get back on their bikes and rejoin the peloton.

Soon after passing through Dozza the peloton slowed, allowing the break to open up the gap to 9 minutes, 15 seconds.

Jonas Abrahamsen was a man on a mission. He made sure he was first over the next two climbs, the fourth-category Côte de Botteghino di Zocca and the third-category Côte de Montecalvo. With 150 of the day's 199 kilometers ridden, on the Montecalvo climb both Primož Roglič's Red Bull-Bora-hansgrohe team and Maxim Van Gils' Lotto Dstny squad hit the front, and with their acceleration the peloton was immediately smaller. Plus, the break's lead was cut in half, to 4 minutes, 15 seconds.

When Abrahamsen went first over the 2 kilometer, 10-percent Côte de San Luca for the first of two trips over the hill, he was still 3 minutes, 25 seconds ahead of the pack. The lead group came apart on that climb, but reassembled on the descent. That cohesion was short-lived. Portuguese racer Neilson Oliveira attacked with 21 kilometers to go and only Abrahamsen and Kevin Vauquelin could stay with him.

The trio circled around for a second ascent of the San Luca climb and there Vauquelin dropped his break partners, building up a lead of 40 seconds. That was the stage. Vauquelin crossed the line alone, 36 seconds ahead of Abrahamsen. Another 15 seconds later Quentin Pacher led in Cristian Rodriguez and Harold Tejada with Oliveira finishing just another second later.

Back in the much-reduced peloton, on the second time up the San Luca, race leader Romain Bardet lost contact and had to watch his chances to retain the Yellow Jersey ride up the hill. Six hundred meters from the top Pogačar accelerated with only Vingegaard able to stay with him. With a kilometer left to climb, Evenepoel and Richard Carapaz were able to regain contact. When that small group crossed the finish line Tadej Pogačar was the race leader with the same elapsed time as Evenepoel, Vingegaard and Carapaz. Romain Bardet dropped to fifth place in the GC, just six seconds behind the lead quartet.

After the stage Pogačar told the press, "In the final circuit I felt super good and the pace was super high already the first time up San Luca because of how the Visma team pulled. Then, the second time, we decided to try so I could test myself a bit.

"Jonas Vingegaard was really quickly on my wheel. I'm not surprised at his level. We cooperated well together, but Remco and Richard did too and came back to our wheels at the very end. The whole circuit in Bologna was super crowded, and the climb was insane! Really unbelievable. It's the cycling we should all love.

"Am I going to keep the Yellow Jersey for long? Well, I prefer to take it day by day and stick to the original plan."

Vingegaard was also very pleased, "It's a small victory for me that I was able to follow Pogačar", Vingegaard responded afterwards. "Beforehand, I thought this stage would be one where I might lose time on the competition. The steep climbs [at the end of] the stage were not my specialty, but I felt good. Pogačar and I immediately decided to work together until the finish. The first two stages went better than expected. I doubted myself. It was difficult to predict how I was going to feel after such a short preparation. I am very happy to be able to say that I am at [a good] level again. Hopefully this is the start of a great three weeks."

The Tour organizers believed the third stage was perfect for the pure sprinters with just three fourth-category climbs, the last one coming about 50 kilometers from the finish. The race was still in Italy, starting in Piacenza (Plaisance in French) and heading west to Turin. The route was well clear of the Alps to the north and avoided the Apennines to the south. At 230.8 kilometers, this was the 2024 Tour's longest stage.

Pogačar would spend the twenty-second day of his pro racing career in Yellow. He was also the first rider in fourteen years to have worn the *Maglia Rosa* of the Giro leader as well and the *Maillot Jaune* of the Tour leader in the same year. The last rider to accomplish this was in 2010 when Cadel Evans put on the Pink Jersey after that Giro's second stage and the Yellow after the eighth stage of the 2010 Tour.

There was a general assumption within the peloton that the sprinters' teams were not going to let this chance get away from them and any breakaway was doomed to being chased down before the finish. Jonas Abrahamsen and a teammate made a quick excursion off the front, but were soon back in the pack.

About a third of the way into the stage, as a tribute to Fausto Coppi, the race passed through the town of Tortona, where the *Campionissimo* lived and is now buried. The race went over the fourth category Côte de Tortone-Fausto Coppi with the tireless Jonas Abrahamsen being first over the hill.

The Alexandrie intermediate sprint at kilometer 94 showed which sprinters had their fast-twitch muscle fibers tuned up. Lidl-Trek's Mads Pedersen won it, beating fastmen Jasper Philipsen and Bryan Coquard.

Local rider Matteo Sobrero was first over the day's second climb, the Côte de Barbaresco. His family and fan club were there waiting for him to celebrate the moment of their boy being at the head of the race.

Not everyone had given upon getting away and on the day's third and last climb Fabien Grellier escaped on the Côte de Sommariva Perno. As he crested the hill he had a 40-second lead. And of course, he was brought back to the fold with 28 kilometers to go.

Things looked to be set up for a giant sprint in Turin. But with a little over two kilometers to go there was a big crash, taking down Jasper Philipsen. His teammate, also a man who can make a bike go blindingly fast, Mathieu van der Poel, flatted near the end. The winner was Biniam Girmay, beating Fernando Gaviria, Arnaud De Lie, Mads Pedersen and Dylan Groenewegen.

Girmay's team noted, "The winner, Biniam Girmay, becomes the first rider from Black Africa to win a stage in the Tour de France, and thus makes cycling history with [Team] Intermarché-Wanty after his resounding successes in Ghent–Wevelgem and the Giro d'Italia."

Girmay, moved by the importance of the moment said, "This is a historic day, I'm so happy for myself, for my Intermarché-Wanty team, but also for my country and my continent. Ever since I was a child, taking part in the Tour de France was a dream, almost unhoped-for. Winning [a stage in] the Tour de France is so incredible, especially in such a competitive sprint."

Richard Carapaz, who finished fourteenth, became the new owner of the Yellow Jersey. He was still tied in GC time with Pogačar, Evenepoel and Vingegaard.

Stage four not only took the Tour over the border and into France, it also sent the riders into this Tour's first high mountains.

On the way to the finish city of Valloire the riders would go over three famous climbs. First, at 50 kilometers into the stage, the riders would go over the 39.9-kilometer second-category Sestrière ascent. Then, just after crossing the border into France came the second-category Col de Montgenèvre and finally, the riders would face one of the Tour's legendary climbs, the *Hors Catégorie* Col du Galibier.

This would be the sixty-third time the Tour had gone over the Galibier, the eighth-highest paved road in the Alps. The Tour first sent riders over the big mountain in 1911. Back then, only three riders were able to ride up the mountain, the rest had to walk their bikes.

The stage started down one rider. A victim of the late stage three crash, Casper Pedersen suffered a fractured collarbone. That left 174 riders on the line to start climbing almost from the gun. Mads Pedersen tried to get away immediately, but he was soon brought back to the pack. He still had enough suds to win the intermediate sprint 19 kilometers into the stage.

Ten kilometers later seventeen riders went clear, among them Stephen Williams, winner of the 2024 Flèche Wallonne classic race in April. Williams was first over both the Sestrière and the Montgenèvre climbs. The peloton with the race favorites went over the Montgenèvre 2 minutes, 10 seconds behind the break.

On the Montgenèvre descent, Pogačar teammate Nils Politt dropped like a rock as he led Pogačar and his teammates down the mountain, splitting the peloton into several groups. Richard Carapaz was timed at 86.6 kilometers an hour in his chase to get back up to the front of the pack. The peloton came together in town of Briançon, at the bottom of the descent. In the valley at the foot of the Galibier the break was 2 minutes, 30 seconds ahead.

On the Galibier the break came apart with only four riders left up front, who refused to work with each other. The UAE Team Emirates-led peloton had also suffered serious attrition, now having only 30 riders.

Six kilometers from the summit Carapaz was dropped and at three kilometers from the top the Yellow Jersey group was down to just eight riders.

Pogačar bided his time and just 800 meters from the summit he jumped, and hard. Evenepoel was quickly dropped. Vingegaard could hold his wheel for about 100 meters and then he too fell back. Pogačar went over the summit 10 seconds ahead of Vingegaard. Being a very capable descender, on the way down to the finish Pogačar increased the gap, growing it to 35 seconds by the time he arrived in Valloire. Evenepoel was second, followed by Juan Ayuso, Primož Roglič and 2 seconds later Vingegaard.

Pogačar was again in Yellow with Evenepoel second at 45 seconds and Vingegaard third at 50 seconds.

Pogačar, was joyous after the stage, "I'm super happy. This was more or less the plan, and we executed it pretty well. It was like a dream stage, and finishing it off solo was very special. I wanted to hit hard today, as I was confident I could win and put some seconds on my rivals.

"I know this stage pretty well. I've trained a lot here and it felt like a home stage, passing through Sestrière and Montgenèvre. There was a lot of headwind in the Galibier climb, so the pace didn't feel that hard when following wheels. Still, my team did a super good job. I didn't want to attack too early because of the wind, so I saved my legs until that attack with 800 meters to go on which I pushed as hard as possible in order to make such big differences possible.

"I knew the downhill, and that helped a lot, but it was a bit scary and surprising to see that the first few corners were wet. The gaps I created are good news for me. I can be happy with the position and the shape I am in right now. Yet there are three demanding weeks ahead of us, and as for this week in particular there is an ITT [individual time trial] that can create some gaps."

The Story of the 2024 Tour de France

Vingegaard was philosophical, "The 50 seconds behind Pogačar in the general classification are playable", Vingegaard responded afterwards. "It's never nice to lose time, but to be honest I expected bigger time differences after four stages. Today I lost most of my time in the second part of the descent. I was 10 seconds behind for some time, but on the long straights he was able to gain seconds. We know what we are doing. We believe in our plan."

At last. After four stages and 775.6 kilometers of racing the sprinters had a stage truly made for them. The day's racing through the mountainous department of Savoy had just two rated ascents, but they were both easier fourth category, one of them 1.5 and the other 3 kilometers long. These were climbs top professional sprinters like Jasper Philipsen and Mark Cavendish can generally handle.

The riders set out from Saint-Jean-de-Maurienne. Because of its proximity to several of the great Alpine passes, the Tour has come to the city several times in recent years. It was the start city for the 2019 Tour's nineteenth stage, famously cut short after a terrible hailstorm and mudslide.

There was some worry at the start: though the riders began the stage on dry roads, it was raining in the tiny finish city of St. Vulbas.

There was the usual tussling during the stage's early kilometers as different combinations of riders tried to get away. It wasn't until 25 kilometers of racing that the pack let a pair of riders get away. First, Groupama-FDJ rider Clement Russo escaped by himself and then 6 kilometers later he was joined by TotalEnergies rider Mattéo Vercher. Forty kilometers into the stage the duo had a 4 minute, 35 second gap. Lidl-Trek and Alpecin-Deceuninck patrolled the front of the peloton and made sure the two fugitives stayed within reach.

On the Côte de Lhuis, the day's second climb 142 kilometers into the stage, rain was falling on the pack, a pack determined to catch the two breakaway riders. And indeed, the pair were caught just as the climb began to bite.

Jonas Abrahamsen was first over the top, collecting another climber's point. He now had enough points to keep the Polka-Dot Jersey for two more days, even if he won no more points.

Approaching the finishing sprint, Jasper Philipsen's Alpecin-Deceuninck team did all they could to set the sprinter up for a stage win, but it was Mark Cavendish who won the stage, with a clear gap between himself and Philipsen. That gave him his thirty-fifth Tour de France stage win, breaking the stage-win tie he had with Eddy Merckx. Mark Cavendish had now won more Tour de France stages than any other rider in Tour history.

After the stage Mark Cavendish said, "It's hard to fully grasp this success, but we worked towards it, and as a team, we did everything possible to make it happen. We have an incredible team, and I have amazing teammates. Throughout not just this Tour de France but all this time, I felt immense support from the entire team, and today we have the moment to celebrate this success together. I am very happy to be part of Astana Qazaqstan Team, where I found friends and, essentially, an incredible family. Today, the team was magnificent, everything was done perfectly, and I managed to win. I believed in success, but the main thing is that the team believed in success, we were on the same wavelength and had a common goal. I received maximum support, and we purposefully worked towards the goal we achieved today"

Biniam Girmay's ninth place was good enough to make him the new owner of the points classification leader's Green Jersey.

Stage six was nearly a straight-shot north from Mâcon in central-eastern France (the Tour noted that it was the hometown of the poet Alphonse de Lamartine) to the Burgundian city of Dijon, which is about 300 kilometers southeast of Paris. With only a single fourth-category climb coming just 10 kilometers into the stage, stage six would be raw meat for the sprinters.

Lidl-Trek rider Mads Pedersen had crashed hard near the end of stage five. Though he was beat up with a painful left shoulder blade, he had no broken bones. So, a bandaged Pedersen was on the start line.

There were still 174 riders in the peloton as they took off from Mâcon, at speed. There were no early escape attempts, just a peloton rocketing down the road. The top contenders were all at the front. Predicted crosswinds had the riders edgy about the possibility of the peloton breaking apart.

Jonas Abrahamsen was a bit off the front as he went over the only climb of the day, the fourth-category Col de Bois Clair. He had company, Cofidis rider Axel Zingle. Zingle tried, but could not beat the determined Abrahamsen to the top. The result of their efforts was a 75-second gap. Realizing the certainty of their getting caught by the fast-moving peloton, they eased their efforts and allowed themselves to be reabsorbed by the pack.

The Story of the 2024 Tour de France

The pack sped along with the main excitement being an attempt by the Lotto Dstny team to split the peloton. That didn't work, but with 81 kilometers to go, as the Tour left the town of Puligny-Montrachet, Team Visma | Lease a bike rider Christophe Laporte was able to force a split. At that moment Mark Cavendish, who surely was dreaming of another stage win that day, flatted.

Pogačar's team had been asleep. When the split occurred, Pogačar was in the front group, but his teammates were not. Ten kilometers later the peloton came back together.

At the Red Kite, signaling a kilometer to go, Alexander Kristoff's Team Uno-X Mobility hit the front. But the Nordic team's ambitions were thwarted when Dylan Groenewegen scooted by everyone to win in a photo finish, very narrowly beating Jasper Philipsen. Biniam Girmay was third across the line.

Not long after the stage finish the judges relegated Philipsen to the back of his group, 107th for irregular sprinting. That made Girmay second in the stage.

The race organizers noted that this was the first stage win by a reigning Dutch road champion since Léon van Bon won Tour stage six (in the city of Tours, interestingly enough) in 2000.

Pogačar finished thirty-fourth, safely buried in the lead group, giving him another day in Yellow.

After the stage Groenewegen said, "It was really close in the end. Before, I said it would be a nice victory in the red, white, and blue jersey [of the Dutch national champion], but in the end it was so close that I couldn't celebrate on the finish line. I know the legs were really good, I know I have a really strong team, but there are other strong sprinters. Yesterday, Mark Cavendish was really strong and today Jasper Philipsen was really hard to beat, but in the end, we got the victory, which is really important for us."

Now it was time for a test of the racers' raw power. Stage seven was a 25.3-kilometer individual time trial between two tiny towns noted for their wine grapes, Nuits-St.-Georges and Gevrey-Chambertin. To get a sense of where the Tour was at this point, the finish town of Gevrey-Chambertin is just 15 kilometers south of Dijon.

Mark Cavendish was the first rider down the start ramp, followed by his teammate Michael Morkov. The next fifty-eight riders started at one-minute intervals in reverse GC order, then the spacing was increased to 1 minute, 30 seconds. The final nine riders started at 2-minute intervals. Pogačar went last, at 5:00 PM.

The day's fastest man was Remco Evenepoel, who rode the 25.3 kilometers in 28 minutes, 52 seconds, an incredible 52.587 kilometers per hour. Pogačar was only 12 seconds slower.

Roglič was in the hunt at 34 seconds, with Vingegaard another 3 seconds slower.

Pogačar remained the GC leader, of course, with Evenepoel second in the GC at 33 seconds and Vingegaard third, at 1 minute, 15 seconds.

Vingegaard was sanguine about the stage, "To be honest, it was a good time trial for me. I'm satisfied with my performance. Especially in the first part of the time trial I felt myself in very good shape. On the climb I was able to pedal with fine power. To only lose 37 seconds compared to Evenepoel, I had signed up for that beforehand. The 25-second difference with Pogačar is also playable. Of course they take time, but I expected to lose more. The course is much more suited to them… As I have already indicated, anything we achieve is nice. Of course we are going for the highest possible, but losing time in the first part of the Tour was definitely calculated. I feel my form is improving day by day."

Mads Pedersen called it quits. He had suffered through the pain and swelling from his stage-five crash, but his team finally decided he needed to quit the race and heal up for the rest of the season.

Stage eight's 183.4 kilometers had five rated climbs, all category three and four. The day's climbs were finished after 122 of the day's 183 kilometers, meaning that if the pack broke up in the hills, a re-grouping in the flat last 60-odd kilometers was likely.

The stage finished in the tiny town of Colombey-les-Deux-Eglises, situated 260 kilometers east-southeast of Paris. After Mads Pedersen's withdrawal from the peloton, there were 173 riders on the start line. While the riders didn't face a truly challenging course, the day's weather looked like it might make up for that. There was rain early in the stage and the wind was blowing from the southwest at 23 kilometers per hour (14 miles per hour).

With the drop of the start flag teammates Neilson Powless and Stefan Bissegger of EF Education-EasyPost along with Jonas Abrahamsen of Uno-X Mobility scooted off the front. They quickly built a gap and just 16 kilometers into the stage they were 2 minutes, 25 seconds ahead of the field.

At the top of the day's first climb after 24 kilometers, the gap had been cut to just 1 minute, 15 seconds. EF Education-EasyPost had wanted to put either Ben Healy or Alberto Bettiol in the break, and seeing that they weren't going to succeed, they not only backed off from pursuing the break, they called Powless and Bissegger back to the pack.

TotalEnergies rider Jordan Jegat tried to get up to the now-solo Abrahamsen, but could not get across the gap to the speeding Norwegian. So, Abrahamsen went over the next two climbs alone and 50 kilometers into the stage he had increased his lead to 5 minutes, 40 seconds.

Pressing on and still alone and off the front, Abrahamsen went over the final two climbs by himself. Given the climber's points up for grabs in the upcoming two stages, he has secured the Polka-Dot Jersey for at least two more days.

With 60 kilometers left, Abrahamsen's lead had shrunk to 4 minutes, and with 14.4 kilometers left he was caught by a peloton of more than 100 riders. A big sprint was in the making.

Biniam Girmay won his second stage this Tour, again outsprinting Jasper Philipsen and Arnaud De Lie. Pogačar had very smartly put himself near the front of the pack and finished thirteenth. There was no change to the top of the GC with Evenepoel second at 33 seconds and Vingegaard still third, 1 minute, 15 seconds down.

When Girmay's Intermarché Wanty team came to the 2024 Tour, they were among the three teams that had never won a Tour de France stage. Now they were the only team in the race that had won more than one stage (stages three and eight).

Stage nine was a tough one. In addition to four fourth-category climbs, the riders would be sent over fourteen sectors totaling 32.2 kilometers of white gravel roads, just like in Italy's Strade Bianche race. While this stage had fourteen sectors and the 2024 edition of Strade Biache had fifteen sectors, the 2024 edition of the Italian semi-classic had almost double the gravel with 71.5 kilometers of *chemins blancs.* But here in the Tour, after eight stages of hard racing, this day would make tired legs cry.

The race was still near Paris, with the stage starting and finishing in the town of Troyes. The riders would be sent southeast in a big loop. The first gravel sector wouldn't be encountered until the forty-seventh kilometer of the stage. The eleven final sections of gravel would all be in the stage's last 94 kilometers.

The start of the stage was delayed. At the Tour of Austria the day before, Norwegian racer Andre Drege died following a crash while descending the Grossglockner pass. It was arranged for the Norwegian team Uno-X Mobility to arrive at the start line five minutes early for a period of silence to mourn the racer's passing.

After several early unsuccessful break attempts, Romain Gregoire, Neilson Powless, Jarrad Drizners, Derek Gee and French champion Paul Lapeira were able to put together a working group, and 20 kilometers into the stage they had a 25-second gap.

That didn't last; they were caught. Then just before the first white road sector, ten riders got away. By the time they exited that gravel sector they had built a 45-second lead.

After the day's first climb, the Côte de Bergères, 52 kilometers into the stage, Axel Zingle and Alex Aranburu made it up to the break. At nearly the same time Powless dropped back to help his teammate Ben Healy (joined by Tom Pidcock) get up to the break. It worked. They made contact just before the second gravel sector, Chemin de Baroville, at kilometer 66.

Vingegaard's Visma | Lease a Bike led the peloton over the Baroville sector. In this group were Pogačar and Evenepoel. Roglič was dropped, but he quickly got back up to the Pogačar group, bringing about thirty riders with him. By the eighty-fourth kilometer the break had a 90-second gap.

Come the next sector, Hautes Forêts, about 97 kilometers into the stage, Vingegaard had a mechanical problem that forced him to trade bikes with teammate Jan Tratnik. With Pogačar's UAE Team Emirates hammering away at the front, Vingegaard needed a bike immediately.

Exiting the next gravel sector Pogačar launched his first attack. Evenepoel and Matteo Jorgenson jumped on his wheel to negate the effort. Things were clearly warming up. At the top of the day's last rated climb and still in the Loches-sur-Ource to Chacenay gravel sector, Evenepoel attacked. He was immediately joined by the watchful Pogačar as well as Vingegaard. Pogačar joined Evenepoel in working hard to help the trio, but Vingegaard refused to help. Still the three went after the break, but it was to no avail. The trio soon sat up, caught by the peloton led by Roglič's Red Bull-Bora-hansgrohe team, who didn't want such a powerful group getting away without their team leader.

Meanwhile, up in the break, there had been an attack that was neutralized. But with 156 kilometers in their legs, a group of seven riders escaped from the pack and took off after the break. In that group were some superb riders, including Biniam Girmay, Mathieu van der Poel, Jakob Fuglsang and Michael Matthews.

Come the Ru de Paradis gravel sector at kilometer 166, the front group was 65 seconds ahead of the seven chasers and 2 minutes, 10 seconds ahead of the peloton. Pogačar tried again to get away, but Visma riders chased him down.

The chase group could not catch the front break. From them Jasper Stuyven put in a huge effort with eleven kilometers to go and opened a gap. He came close. He was caught in the final kilometer with TotalEnergies rider Anthony Turgis beating Tom Pidcock and Derek Gee to win the stage.

A big group with Pogačar and the rest of the GC contenders came in 1 minute, 46 seconds later, led in by Pascal Ackermann.

After the stage Remco Evenepoel said, "I felt good today, stayed the whole time out of trouble thanks to a very good team, and at one moment I decided to attack on one of the sectors, despite being some 80 kilometers from the finish. It's a pity that some didn't work in the group, as we could have gained a significant margin of minutes even over the others, but it was their tactic in the end, so we have to accept it, that's cycling.

"Personally, I did a good stage, had fun out there and proved that I can ride on the gravel. It's a nice way to conclude what has been a strong and rewarding first week of the Tour de France for us. I am satisfied with how things stand, the shape and the confidence are there, so everything that comes from now on will be a bonus."

The GC on July 7, after nine stages and before the first rest day:

1. Tadej Pogačar: 35hours, 42minutes, 42seconds
2. Remco Evenepoel @ 33 seconds
3. Jonas Vingegaard @ 1 minute, 15 seconds
4. Primož Roglič @ 1 minute, 36 seconds
5. Juan Ayuso @ 2 minutes, 16 seconds

The peloton had covered 1,524.2 kilometers at an average speed of 42.681 kilometers per hour.

Let's pause for a moment and see what David and Aaron Stanley have to say about the Tour's first week:

David wrote:

You wanted a Tour with lots to love, lots of surprises, lots of excitement, right? Week One reminds us that no matter how convinced we are of the Tour's outcome (I plead guilty to that one), the 176 men we *call Les Forçats de la Route* will surprise and please the hell out of us, *Les Forçats de la Sofa.*

A Bunch of Things that I Loved (in no particular order) This Past Week (and a couple that really frosted my cookies!):

1. Biniam Girmay (Intermarché–Wanty). I want to brag on this man from Eritrea. He was the first Black man, and the first Black African, to win a stage. He was also the first to wear the Green Jersey. He was the first man to win two stages in the 2024 Tour. Extraordinary, what this means. Several years ago, I co-authored a biography about a Black man named Willie Artis, born in the Jim Crow South in 1935, who rose to prominence as a wealthy industrialist and Black business counselor to President Obama. Willie told me stories about what it was like to be a Black kid in 1947 and watch Jackie Robinson break MLB's color barrier. I can't hope enough that a whole bunch of young boys and girls on the African continent see what Biniam is doing, and reach for his level of stardom.

   I also see Girmay shifting from a wicked good sprinter into a classics rider a la Laurent Jalabert. He's that talented, *mais bien sûr.*
2. Richard Carapaz (EF Education-EasyPost) was the first Ecuadorian to take the *maillot jaune.* It was day of smart riding, grit, and some brio, eh?
3. The first seven stages, we saw seven different winners. Never boring that way, *d'accord*?
4. Romain Bardet (Team dsm–firmenich PostNL) is a brave and daring rider. An exceptional climber with a Climber's Jersey in the 2019 Tour de France and two podium appearances, he is, much like Raymond Poulidor, beloved by his country's fans. To see him take the first stage so bravely, in his last Tour de France (he's announced he's retiring next spring, most likely after Paris–Nice) made a fair few French unleash their optical waterworks.

5. French rider Kévin Vauquelin (Arkéa–B&B Hotels) won the day in stage two, making it back-to-back days with a French rider winning the stage. It's not a rarity: French riders won back-to-back stages in the Tour de France in 2023 with a stage two win by Victor Lafay followed by Julian Alaphilippe's stage three victory the next day. They also won back-to-back in 2020. On July 14, Bastille Day, Nans Peters won stage eight, followed by Julian Alaphilippe's victory on stage nine the next day. It is important to rejoice with the French. After all, it's been thirty-nine years since Bernard Hinault won the Tour in 1985.

6. The name is Remco. Remco Evenepoel. I ride for Soudal Quick-Step. That's right: say my name. I am the world champion time trialist. I have won stages in all three Grand Tours by the age of twenty-four. I am the greatest threat to the Tadej Pogačar/UAE Team Emirates hegemony in this year's Tour de France. I shall gaze down upon you from the podium. From what step, it is still undetermined, for my two rivals are also strong and battle-tested. I shall fight with the wisdom and intensity of an indomitable warrior and we will see who stands alone on the podium's top step. [DS: I may have gotten a little carried away there, but this is going to be an incredible battle.]

7. Primož Roglič (Red Bull-Bora-hansgrohe). The man is a very canny rider. There is only one way he can win and that is to play the long game. At thirty-four, he cannot waste any energy. With three weeks of racing, you cannot burn a single extra match. Yet, he waits. He stays close. He stays upright. He needs to be a stoic, reserving his *ki* for that one telling moment, his dire opening into the maelstrom that are Tadej and Remco. Come week three, he sees his chance, buries himself, opens a gap, and he just may find himself on the podium.

8. Tadej, Jonas, and Remco. In my preview, I made them the podium. I don't see that changing. These three are truly generational talents. It has been many years since we have seen three riders so closely aligned with talent, discipline, and good sportsmanship. Remco and Tadej greeted each other during the post-time trial warm-down. Respect all the way round. Did you see Riis hugging it out with Indurain in 1996? Or Greg and Bernie in 1986? Yeah, me neither.

9. Frosted cookies. A heads-up for riders in the Tour de France: while you are out of the race course, avoid all affectionate behavior. Julien Bernard (Lidl-Trek) was fined 200 Swiss francs (231 American dollars) by the UCI after stopping to kiss his wife and son during the stage seven time trial of the Tour de France. Around the 15-minute mark of Friday's time trial, Bernard's wife and two-year-old son were on the road with other family members when he pulled over to greet them. The UCI didn't think that show of affection was cute, speaking in a statement of Bernard's "unseemly or inappropriate behavior during the race and damage to the image of the sport." Bernard's response to the blazered idiocy of the UCI was pure and lovely: "Sorry, but what was that? I love you so much. I'm sorry UCI for damaging the image of the sport," Bernard said in a message posted on X. "But I'm willing to pay 200 Swiss francs every day and experience this moment again." Bernard finished the stage in sixty-first place, 3 minutes, 11 seconds behind Remco Evenepoel, the stage winner.

My message to the UCI: Dear massive asshatted Blazers—instead of worrying about a team's workhorse greeting his family in what for Bernard was a meaningless stage, how about you once again take action to ensure safe sprinting areas during the last 5 kilometers, adequate marking and warning about road dividers and traffic furniture and let's ignore tall socks and families who might have this once in a lifetime opportunity to greet Dad/brother/hubs on the job. You want to talk about "unseemly behavior"? Take a look in your collective mirrors, UCI, and you'll see the fountain of all sporting unseemly behavior. Okay, rant over.

10. Cav. Project Thirty-Five, level achieved. Astana Qazaqstan Team came to this Tour, this season! with only one goal—get Cav his thirty-fifth Tour de France stage win and forever see their name attached to the name of the greatest sprinter in Tour de France history. (No, he's not the Greatest of ALL-TIME!, that's still Eddy. Cav, and pretty much every single one of cycling's cognoscenti acknowledge this gladly.)

His thirty-fifth win was a wild one. His lead-out man, Michael Morkov, is the best in the business and got Cav into the madness. Along the way, Mads Pedersen (Lidl-Trek) crashed at near 40 mph at the left side barricade. Axel Zingle (Cofidis), leading out teammate

Bryan Coquard, bunny-hopped right over Pedersen, saving the Dane a nice set of broken ribs and at 30 miles per hour, had the presence to look around and see where his sprinter was. But wait, there's more! As Cav coasted the last 2-3 bike lengths over the line, arms in the air, his chain (as often happens to Mark—I have this on good authority from famed cycling photographer John Pierce) hopped right off the chainring. Yes, Cav finished the stage with both a win and an unrideable bike. A pro's pro, *bien sûr*.

Cav turned pro in 2004 for Team Sparkasse at age twenty-three. He broke out in 2008 with four Tour stage wins for T-Mobile. He's won World Track championships. He's won Classics and Monuments. He's medaled in the Olympics, won the Green Jersey in the Tour, the Points Jersey in the Giro, and seventeen stages, the Points Jersey and four stages in the Vuelta. As Mark has often said, "I'm not just a sprinter. I'm a really good bike racer."

Indeed, you are, Mr. Cavendish. *Chapeau.*

Note: I wrote the above the evening of July 6, after Saturday's stage eight. By noon, July 7, some things happened:

Stage nine. Sunday's stage nine was the single best day of road racing in 2024. Not "in the Tour so far," but all year, from the January startup races until today, July 7. It was truly a battle royale. We use that phrase a lot but few know what a true battle royale is. In the nineteen-teens and the Roaring Twenties, boxing promoters would hire a dozen or more boxers, throw them all into the ring simultaneously, hoist a big bag of money over the boxing ring, and then ring the bell to start the madness. It was every man for himself, attacks came from behind, beside, and everywhere else. You might be trading blows with a guy, and someone would creep up beside you and clobber the side of your head. You fought until you got knocked out, and then, they'd drag you out of the ring. The last man standing would stumble out of the ring with a bag of money, all the change that spectators ringside would toss into the ring, and all the brain damage he could carry.

That was today's stage. Fourteen sectors of gravel which totaled around 32 kilometers. More importantly for the fans, we got to watch TWO battles royale: the group up front from which Anthony Turgis (TotalEnergies) took the win, and the GC group, who are racing for the Big Win in Nice. Kudos to Primož, who was in a battle for his GC life all day, and never blinked, and Tadej, who was willing to lose today in order to attack, attack, attack to earn a few more minutes over Remco and Jonas.

Today, the entire peloton showed they have earned tomorrow's rest day. Me? I felt like I needed a shower after watching the stage.

Aaron wrote:

Week one of the 2024 Tour de France was a scriptwriter's dream. A long-suffering contender gets his day in the *maillot jaune*; a young star catapults himself to the top; one of the all-time greats breaks a historic record—try to make a movie out of this week and Hollywood might tell you that your story is too unbelievable. And yet believable it must be, writ large in full color before our eyes. Here's a look back at some of the best parts of the first week of the 111th *Grande Boucle*.

–Romain Bardet gets his day in the limelight

It was a sure thing that Bardet would seek glory this year after announcing it would be his final Tour. Though it seemed more likely that he would wait for the mountains before attempting to take a stage victory, stage one offered an enticing array of climbs straight out of the gate in Florence, and Team dsm-firmenich PostNL took full advantage, as Bardet and Frank van den Broek struck out on a nearly 50-kilometer adventure together, culminating with the two crossing the finish line mere meters ahead of the charging peloton. For Bardet, this meant putting on the sacred Yellow Jersey for the first time in a career that has spanned over a decade of competition at his home country's most famous race, one where he came ever so close, year after year, to achieving one of the ultimate goals in the sport.

It was pure joy for him and for his supporters, as his "ultimate dream" was finally brought to reality. Though he will not ever win a Tour, he will leave an indelible mark on the race, winning multiple stages, finishing on the podium twice, and with six top-ten finishes to his name. Bardet's name will be etched among a pantheon of French greats when all is said and done in his career.

–Girmay's ascension

Before 2024, the only African country to produce a Tour de France stage winner was South Africa. That all changed on stage three, as Eritrea's Biniam Girmay—brought to the Tour ostensibly as a leadout man for Gerben Thijssen—charged to the win. It was the first win for a Black African cyclist in the Tour de France, two years after he accomplished the same feat in the Giro d'Italia, and was achieved at the fore of a veritable who's-who of sprinters in this year's competition. In winning two of the first nine stages, Girmay was incredibly impressive in every regard and his potential seems nearly limitless as he has a solid Intermarche-Wanty roster around him, a nose for choosing the right line, and is even able to compete on classics-style stages as evidenced by his tenth place finish on stage nine on the gravel.

It is exciting to watch him race, and he represents the growth of African cycling in exemplary fashion—witness the videos of excited fans in his hometown of Asmara for an idea of the love that his country has for him. His hold on the Green Jersey is, at the moment, quite firm, and if he can hang on through the next two weeks and wear Green into Nice? What an incredible result it would be!

–Abrahamsen the Unrelenting

There are years where the *supercombatif* prize seems like something of an afterthought, handed out to one of a handful of riders who've exhibited some amount of aggression or other in joining breakaways and chasing stage wins. Through the first week this year, though, Jonas Abrahamsen has put his stamp on the combativity competition in a manner rarely seen before. By now the story of how he put on twenty kilos to switch from a true climber to a *rouleur* is well known, and he has put the additional power to incredible use this year, spending hundreds of kilometers out in breakaways and maintaining an early advantage in the Polka-Dot Jersey standings for good measure. Abrahamsen has been easily the most exciting rider to watch on multiple stages so far, with a presence in the breakaway day in and day out that makes one wonder if he even has to spend a moment thinking about whether to attack the peloton or if the attacks just happen on their own. Abrahamsen displays pure *ciclismo*, and it's a joy to watch.

–Cavendish and the magic of #3

Mark Cavendish and Astana Qazaqstan came into this year's Tour for one reason and one reason only: to seek his thirty-fifth stage win to set the all-time record. In stage five, it happened. Winning in Saint-Vulbas, Cav displayed all of the skills that have become his hallmark over his years in the peloton: his team brought him to the front, he found the exact right wheel to follow and chose the right line in the final meters before exploding with an age-defying acceleration to defeat Jasper Philipsen at the line. If this was to be the final stage he'll ever win, it made for a perfect encapsulation of what has made him the most successful sprinter the Tour has ever seen, and the amount of congratulations and goodwill that poured forth from around the cycling world in the wake of his victory showed how much respect and adoration the Manx Missile has earned in his career.

–The Four Bikesmen of the GCpocalypse

Pogačar. Vingegaard. Roglič. Evenepoel. For the first time, these four arrive at a Grand Tour to compete against one another, and while they came into the Tour in varying levels of form and fitness, they have dispelled any concerns by separating themselves from the pack, holding the four top spots on GC and looking unlikely to give them up. Any concerns over Vingegaard's fitness were allayed in stage two, when Pogačar put a brutal attack on the last ascent of San Luca and Vingegaard held his wheel the entire way. Though Pogačar would go on to solo to victory on stage four after an intense pair of attacks at the top of the Galibier, his three primary rivals came together on the descent and limited their losses, while Evenepoel gained ground on all three of the others on stage seven's individual time trial. The most exciting moments on GC are yet to come in this race, but if the first week of riding is any indication, these four great champions will remain the ones to watch as the Tour wends its way toward its crescendo in week three.

–Gravel, Dust, and Drama

Riders and fans alike had stage nine circled on their calendars, with its fourteen sections of gravel roads sure to create high drama, and it absolutely delivered. Attack after attack came throughout the stage's 199 kilometers. Between the early breakaway, the chasing attacks, or even the top four members of the overall standings driven by Pogačar heading out on a blistering offensive together, this stage featured nonstop excitement. When the proverbial dust finally settled at end of the day, it was Anthony Turgis atop the podium as the stage victor. And while there were no major changes on the GC, the stage succeeded in flying colors in showing the world why the Tour needs to continue putting together profiles like it.

With nine days of utterly gripping racing in the books, the peloton receives a welcome rest day in Orleans before embarking on week two, a gradually ramping set of stages culminating with two high mountain endeavors that may prove decisive: the back-to-back mountaintop finishes at Pla d'Adet and the Plateau de Beille on Saturday and Sunday. There are opportunities for all types of racers in stages ten through fifteen, and the stage is set for another tumultuous six days of racing to come!

Chapter 5
Week Two: Vingegaard rises to the challenge

After spending the rest day in the ancient city of Orléans, about 120 kilometers southwest of Paris, the riders saddled up for stage ten, a nearly due-south 165 kilometer trek to Saint-Amand-Montrond. The road to what is about the geographic center of France was quite flat with no rated ascents. The fear at the start of the stage was of crosswinds and a day spent in echelons.

Red Bull-Bora-hansgrohe rider Aleksandr Vlasov was not on the start line. In a stage nine crash he had fractured his ankle.

There seemed to no rush to get back into battle mode. The peloton rode just 37 kilometers the first hour. The intermediate sprint came 57 kilometers into the stage and caused a bit of a speed-up. Intermarché-Wanty's Kobe Goossens won it, but then peloton quickly regrouped.

The feared crosswinds weren't strong enough disrupt the peloton's progress and come the finish line there were still 138 riders together to contest the stage win. Mathieu van der Poel led out his Alpecin-Deceuninck teammate Jasper Philipsen, who did his job and won the stage. Biniam Girmay and Pascal Ackermann were second and third. The riders had picked up the pace with the average speed for the stage a respectable 43.21 kilometers per hour.

Vingegaard and Pogačar finished twenty-eighth and twenty-ninth, safely buried in the front group.

After the stage Vingegaard's Sports Director Grischa Niermann was already looking ahead to the challenging eleventh stage. "Tomorrow will be a tough stage with more than four thousand altimeters. The succession of climbs in the last fifty kilometers will be grueling. There is a chance for the breakaway, because a stage like this is hard to control. It is a stage that should suit Jonas Vingegaard, but he is logically looking forward more to the stages in the Pyrenees and the Alps. There are the stages that suit him the best."

Stage ten's southward trek had brought the race to the Massif Central, highlands in south-central France that cover about 15 percent of the country. That meant the riders would do some climbing. The bumpy day had six rated climbs, starting with a fourth category hill about 80 kilometers into the stage. The climbing grew more intense in the stage's later kilometers with two second-category ascents and the first-category Puy Mary Pas de Peyrol at the stage's kilometer 180. And there were still two more hills after that.

Tour Boss Christian Prudhomme summed it up, "There's only one stage across the rugged Massif Central, but what a stage it is! With 4,350 meters of vertical gain, the riders will have to be on their mettle at all times, and particularly in the final 50 kilometers, when the degree of difficulty rises a level with a series of very challenging obstacles: the climb to the Col de Néronne, then to the Puy Mary Pas de Peyrol with its fearsome final 2 kilometers, then continuing on to the Col de Pertus, the Col de Font de Cère and the ascent to Le Lioran. They provide all manner of opportunities for eager climbers to attack."

Such a hilly stage cried for a breakaway. Anticipating just that possibility, after two hours the pack had raced across France at more than 47 kilometers per hour. Two ill riders from Cofidis, Ion Izagirre and Alexis Renard, couldn't take the pace and had to abandon.

Finally, on the first rated climb, the fourth-category Côte de Mouilloux, Richard Carapaz and Mattéo Vercher were able to get away. Others were able to bridge up to them and 100 kilometers into the stage there was now a break of ten riders a bit more than 2 minutes ahead of the pack.

The pace took its toll. As the peloton approached the day's third climb, the second-category Col de Néronne, both Romain Bardet and Geraint Thomas were left behind.

Up front, on the first-category Puy Mary Pas de Peyrol, the break had three riders, Oier Lazcano, Richard Carapaz and Ben Healy, with a lead of about 30 seconds. The reduced chasing pack was having none of that. One-by one they were caught, with Healy the last to be absorbed. He was reeled in one kilometer from the summit by what was left of the main group, now a ten-man chasing pack.

Six hundred meters from the top and 32 kilometers from the finish Pogačar attacked. At the top he was 5 seconds ahead of Vingegaard. On the way down he put his superb descending skills to work and grew the gap to a half-minute. On the second-category Col de Pertus, fifteen kilometers from the finish, Vingegaard caught him near the top. Pogačar was still first over the summit, taking a precious 8-second time bonus along the way. Evenepoel grabbed third place.

There was still third-category Col de Font de Cère just 3 kilometers from the finish. The trio remained together and then sprinted for the line. Vingegaard was able outsprint Pogačar for the stage win. Twenty-five seconds later Evenepoel grabbed third place.

Roglič was riding with Evenepoel when the former crashed with 1.1 kilometers to go. He quickly remounted and finished 55 seconds behind Vingegaard. But he was saved by the 3-kilometer rule. If a rider crashes 3 kilometers or less from the line he gets the same time as the group he was with. His finishing time was adjusted to be the same as Evenepoel's.

After the stage Vingegaard said, "This is an emotional win for me. This win means a lot to me. Everything I went through in the past few months is now coming back. The period after my crash in Itzulia Basque Country was tough. It's a victory for my family. They have always been by my side."

He continued, "I couldn't follow Pogačar's attack on the Puy Mary, although I certainly didn't have a big gap up top. I just had to keep fighting and find my own pace. On the descent, he managed to gain some time, so I wasn't expecting to be able to come back. It ended up being a narrow sprint, but I immediately felt the victory was mine. Three months ago I could not have imagined this."

Stage twelve had a somewhat lumpy exit from the Massif Central, though there were only three rated climbs in the stage, all category four, with the last one finishing 135 kilometers into the 203-kilometer stage. The route headed west-southwest for the Tour's upcoming appointment with the Pyrenees.

There were several attempts to form breakaways, but nothing worked until Groupama-FDJ rider Valentin Madouas got a gap after about 19 kilometers of racing. Along with teammate Quentin Pacher, the usual suspects were quickly on his wheel, Jonas Abrahamsen and Anthony Turgis.

Sadly, Fabio Jakobsen and Pello Bilbao, both ill, had to abandon.

As the break went over two of the day's climbs, Abrahamsen made sure he was first to the top. Though he lost the lead in the climber's competition to Pogačar the day before, he was wearing the Polka-Dots, since Pogačar was busy looking good in Yellow.

Abrahamsen was also first over the day's third and final climb at kilometer 135, with the peloton just 70 seconds back. First Turgis was caught by the peloton and then the other three were also brought back to the fold. It looked like there would be a big sprint. As the pack zoomed to the finish city of Villeneuve-sur-Lot, Alexey Lutsenko crashed with 12.5 kilometers to go, bringing down several other riders, including Primož Roglič. This was too far from the finish for Roglič to get that same finishing time as his group.

The stage finish came down to a 68-man sprint, won by Biniam Girmay, who took his third stage win this Tour. Wout van Aert and Arnaud Démare were second and third.

Roglič finished 120th, at 2 minutes, 27 seconds. At the line he was surrounded by Red Bull-Bora-hansgrohe teammates Bob Jungels, Marco Haller, Matteo Sobrero, Danny Van Poppel, and Nico Denz. But now Roglič was sixth in the GC, 4 minutes, 42 seconds behind Pogačar. Moving past the other gifted athletes ahead of him in the GC would be no easy matter.

In fact he couldn't. Overnight Roglič's Red Bull-Bora-hansgrohe team assessed his condition and in the morning decided that he could not continue the Tour. Roglič's exit forced the team to abandon the goal of having him finish with a high GC placing to instead chasing stage wins with other members of the team. Team boss Rolf Aldag said, "We have six world class riders here and the Tour de France is not over until Nice. We have to reset, out of respect for the race, out of respect because all these riders have spent ten weeks away from home preparing. We should not give up! But we should set new goals."

The race needed one more jump south to reach the Pyrenees. Stage thirteen was surely going to be another sprinters' fest with just two fourth-category climbs in its 165.3 kilometers.

There was more attrition. Cofidis rider Jesus Herrada was sick and did not start. Plus, Alpecin-Deceuninck's Jonas Rickaert and Soren Kragh Andersen, as well as Alexey Lutsenko of Astana Qazaqstan, fell outside the time limit when they finished stage twelve, eliminating them from the race. That left 160 riders on the start line.

Part way into the stage Juan Ayuso, sick with Covid-19, abandoned. That meant two riders in the GC top ten (Ayuso and Roglič) had quit the race that day.

Right at the referee's start signal the breakaway attempts started. Very quickly there was a group of twenty-three riders with a gap. But Adam Yates was in that break and since with Roglič's withdrawal he was now sitting in seventh place in the GC at 6 minutes, 59 seconds, Team Visma | Lease a Bike felt the break should be caught. In strong crosswinds the team attacked, with five of their riders accelerating hard. Only a few riders from other teams could go with the move: Almeida, Pogačar, Evenepoel, Campenaerts and Ackermann.

To make the move still more powerful, Jan Tratnik dropped back from the break to assist his teammates.

Team INEOS Grenadiers responded to the danger and 33 kilometers into the stage, Visma's attackers were caught. With the stage's first hour being raced at more than 48 kilometers per hour, the initial break had a gap of just about a minute. It was this high speed racing that forced the ailing Ayuso's abandonment.

In the break Uno-X's Magnus Cort became restive and attacked, taking with him Michal Kwiatkowski, Julian Bernard and Romain Gregoire. Twenty kilometers later the four had a 55-second lead over the big break and another 15 seconds on the peloton. The peloton persisted and 96 kilometers into the stage the original break was caught with the Gregoire quartet still off the front.

Visma | Lease a Bike was feeling its oats that day and with 104 kilometers raced the team attacked again. This broke up the peloton. Adam Yates was the only top rider to miss being in the attacking group, but it all came together, with even the four-man break being caught with 50 kilometers to go.

Come the day's two fourth-category climbs Tobias Halland Johannessen and Richard Carapaz tried to escape but they were absorbed with 21 kilometers left. There were other short-lived attempts to escape but it was clear that the sprinters' teams were in charge.

Despite a crash near the end that took down several riders, including Arnaud de Lie and Amaury Capiot, the stage came down to a big sprint won by Jasper Philipsen with Wout van Aert, Pascal Ackermann and Biniam Girmay taking second through fourth places. Ever watchful, Pogačar was ninth in the stage.

The Tour had promised a weekend to remember and here it was. On Saturday the thirteenth the Tour would tackle the first of two days in the Pyrenees. The day's three climbs were packed into the second half of the 151.9 -kilometer stage.

The first obstacle was the legendary Col du Tourmalet. The Tourmalet has been used in the Tour more than any other pass, starting in 1910 when the Tour went into the Pyrenees for its first trip into high mountains. The Tour wrote that this would be the eightieth time Tour riders would be sent up the *Hors Catégorie* ascent, 19 kilometers averaging 7.4 percent.

Thirty kilometers later the second-category Hourquette d'Ancizan would crossed before the finale, a hilltop finish at the Pla d'Adet ski resort, just above the town of Saint-Lary-Soulan. Also a *Hors Catégorie* climb, the Pla d'Adet climb was 10.6 kilometers long with a gradient 7.9 percent. The finish line was placed exactly where it was when Raymond Poulidor won stage sixteen of the 1974 Tour, 1 minute, 49 seconds ahead of an exhausted Eddy Merckx. Merckx did win the Tour that year, his fifth and final Tour victory.

Experiencing symptoms of Covid-19, Ineos Grenadiers rider Tom Pidcock did not start. Guillaume Boivin of the Israel-Premier Tech team was also ill and did not begin the stage. That left 157 riders to head into the thin air of the high mountains.

The attacks went off almost from the gun and almost immediately stage thirteen crash victim Amaury Capiot was off the back. Unable to keep up with the peloton, in tears, he abandoned.

Thirty-seven kilometers into the stage as the pack passed through the city of Lourdes, Mathieu van der Poel, Bryan Coquard, Cedric Beullens and Arnaud de Lie got clear of the pack. Fourteen kilometers later four more riders joined the break, making eight men off the front.

The day was hot with aggression. Not long after the second group of four joined the break another fifteen riders went clear. As they passed through the town of Esquieze-Sere, 70 kilometers into the stage, the gap between the two breaks was only 30 seconds, with the pack now four minutes behind.

As the Tourmalet reared up, there were seventeen riders off the front. Near the top David Gaudu and Oier Lazkano sprinted off to claim the climber's points. Lazkano was first, 12 seconds ahead of Gaudu.

At the foot of the next climb, the Hourquette d'Ancizan, the now five escapees were about three minutes ahead of the pack. This time Gaudu was first over, with the peloton 1 minute, 15 seconds back. The break had lost more than a minute and a half on the ascent.

The now five breakaways, Kwiatkowski, Gaudu, Healy, Lazkano and Meintjes began the hard climb to the finish. Healy went solo early in the climb. From the peloton Adam Yates attacked with 7 kilometers to go and two kilometers later Pogačar took off. Together, the two passed Healy. Vingegaard and Evenepoel went after the front riders and passed Yates.

Pogačar crossed the line alone with Vingegaard coming in second 39 seconds later. Evenepoel was third, at 1 minute, 19 seconds.

Vingegaard was now second in the GC, 1 minute, 57 seconds down and Evenepoel was third, at 2 minutes, 22 seconds.

Unbowed, Vingegaard looked back on the stage with mixed feelings. "I am satisfied with my own performance, but at the same time of course disappointed with the time loss. This is Tadej's territory, but of course I would have preferred not to have lost any time today. On the steep sections of the climb I felt like I was getting closer and closer. However, the final kilometers were right up Tadej's alley, given the power he has. He deserved the stage win today. I am already looking forward to tomorrow. It will be climbing from the start. It will be a long, grueling day. Those days usually suit me. Together with the strong team I have around me, we will do everything we can to make it a success. The battle is definitely not over yet."

Bastille Day, July 14, would be celebrated by sending the riders over as tough a route as can be conceived. At the gun the riders would begin climbing the first-category Col de Peyresourde, 6.9 kilometers of 7.8 percent gradient. The Peyresourde was one of the first climbs included in that 1910 Tour's first trip in the mountains. The organizers like it and as of this writing has been climbed in the Tour about seventy times. Its position in the Pyrenees make it a natural crossing point to other climbs and finish points.

From there the hits kept coming. After the Peyresourde came three famous and well-used first-category ascents: Col de Menté, Col du Portet d'Aspet, and the Col d'Agnes. After the Col d'Agnes the riders would descend a bit and climb the unrated Port de Lers.

Then, the finale: 15.8 kilometers of 7.9 percent *Hors Catégorie* gradient to the finish at Plateau de Beille. The sprinters would likely take almost an hour to trickle in after the men with wings crossed the line. Tour boss Christian Prudhomme noted that the day had 4,850 meters of vertical gain.

It was a warm day, 30°C (85°F) with a light breeze from the north as the riders headed up into the clouds. As usual, the attacks flew off at the start. Nothing stuck. David Gaudu was first over the Peyresourde with Oier Lazkano and Romain Bardet joining him on the descent. The trio was soon caught.

At about the bottom of the descent Bob Jungels started attacking. He kept at it all the way up to the top of the Col de Mente. Still, Javier Romo beat him to the summit. About seventeen riders formed up on the descent. They built a 1 minute, 35 second lead over the Visma | Lease a Bike-led peloton.

Next up at kilometer 65 was the first-category Col de Portet d'Aspet another venerable climb that was also part of that 1910 Tour. Since 1947 it has been used in the Tour thirty-six times. Seventeen riders got a gap on the big mountain with Norwegian rider Tobias Halland Johannessen cresting the mountain first. At this point the peloton was just 65 seconds back.

With almost 70 kilometers between the peaks of the Col de Portet d'Aspet and the next climb, the first-category Col d'Agnes, the break was able to grow its lead to 3 minutes, 30 seconds before the hard climbing began. The break came apart on the ascent with Laurens De Plus first over. The Yellow Jersey group, still led by Visma | Lease a Bike, was down to just fifteen riders.

Come the day's last climb to Plateau de Beille, a group of five were away: Laurens De Plus, Jai Hindley, Enric Mas, Richard Carapaz, and Tobias Halland Johannessen. The quintet was 2 minutes, 25 seconds ahead of the GC group.

Inevitably the lead group came apart on the brutal climb with Mas and Carapaz the last to be caught by the relentless Vingegaard-led group.

With 11 kilometers to go Vingegaard attacked and Pogačar was immediately on his wheel. Vingegaard led the duo up the mountain and away from everyone else. And then the completely expected happened. With 5.4 kilometers to go Pogačar attacked and took off up the road for another solo victory. In those short 5.4 kilometers he took 1 minute, 8 seconds out of Vingegaard. Evenepoel came in third, at 2 minutes, 51 seconds.

The Story of the 2024 Tour de France

Now came rest day two before an incredible week of mountain racing. So far the 2024 Tour had visited the Apennines, the Italian and (a little of) the French Alps as well as the Massif Centrale. Next up, the Tour would head east for some real time in the Alps, starting with stage seventeen.

The GC after stage sixteen:

1. Tadej Pogačar: 61 hours, 56 minutes, 24 seconds
2. Jonas Vingegaard @ 3 minutes, 9 seconds
3. Remco Evenepoel @ 5 minutes, 19 seconds
4. Joao Almeida @ 10 minutes 54 seconds
5. Mikel Landa @ 11 minutes 21 seconds

The Tour had so far covered 2,641 kilometers at an average speed of 42.638 kilometers per hour.

Let's pause and see what David and Aaron Stanley had to say about week two:

David wrote:

Stage ten: Alpecin-Deceuninck's Mathieu van der Poel proved he could win mass sprints when he did a lead-out that found his sprinter Jasper Philipsen struggling to hold onto MvdP's wheel as the sprint wound up with 200 meters to go. We, as fans, also found that relegation penalties work as somehow, Jasper managed to sprint in a straight line for the first time in this Tour to nab his stage win over Green Jersey hero Biniam Girmay (Intermarché-Wanty).

Stage eleven: All of cycling wondered about Jonas (Visma | Lease a Bike). Did he come to the Tour to test his fitness, recover his fitness, play spoiler and chase after mountain stage victories, or to win the race? He was horribly injured, he said he felt close to death, and his tears of joy after he outsprinted breakaway buddy Tadej were real. This is now *mano a mano* for the 2024 Tour de France. The only way this race could now be more compelling is if one of them showed up on the start line wearing a black mask over his eyes, and the other said "My name is Inigo Montoya. You killed my father. Prepare to die."

Stage twelve: The nine fastest men in this year's Tour were all outkicked by the World's Fastest Sprinter, 2024 edition. Biniam Girmay

(Intermarché-Wanty) took his third stage win over a stellar field. Twelve stages, three stage wins, the *maillot vert*? So far, so good for the national hero of Eritrea. Yes, a national hero like we rarely see. I checked out an Eritrean newspaper, *Tesfa News* and found that six of the seven lead articles were on Biniam. The seventh was a small piece about a new Italian-Eritrean strategic business partnership. The story of Eritrea is all-Biniam, all the time. And well-earned by Mr. Girmay. Kudos.

On a sad note, it looked as if Primož Roglič (Red Bull-Bora-hans-grohe) was doing everything right. Staying close, reserving his energy, riding smart. And then, Bam! Down goes Primož! Down goes Primož! Down goes Primož! [said in a Howard Cosell-like boxing commentator voice calling the iconic Frazier–Foreman heavyweight championship bout in 1973.]

Roglič would finish the stage, but was a DNS on the morning of Friday's Stage thirteen. The latter stages of Primož Roglič's career now resemble the classic Albert King blues song, *Born Under a Bad Sign*:

> Born under a bad sign
> Been down since I begin to crawl
> If it wasn't for bad luck
> You know I wouldn't have no luck at all

Stage fourteen: Yes, stage fourteen was slated to be an epic stage, what with the Tourmalet ("Assassins!" yelled stage winner Octave Lapize at the race organizers during the tenth stage of the 1910 Tour de France, as he crested the dreaded Tourmalet) and the Souvenir Jacques Goddet and the final rush up the Pla d'Adet, where Ben Healey (EF Education-EasyPost) had his stage winning dream crushed by the most dominant Grand Tour rider we've seen this century on what might have been his most dominant day. Poor Ben, yet looked at ob-jectively, Jonas had an exceptional ride. Our Tadej, his ride was be-yond HC.

But you know all that because you're a fan. Let's talk about Sean Quinn (EF Education-EasyPost). Quinn is a SoCal kid, twenty-four years old, and has had a darned fine journeyman's career since turning pro in 2020 as a *stagiaire* with Deceuninck Quick-Step and full-time pro with EF Education in 2022. But since taking the US National Pro Champs in Charleston, WV, Sean's quality has shown as brightly as the gaudy stars and stripes jersey he pulled on that day. Whenever possible on the flat, Sean has sneaked into the breakaway. But that's not his strong suit. His strong suit? Whenever the road has tilted up, Sean has been in the breakaway. Young Mr. Quinn, like Mr. Jorgenson and Mr. Kuss and Mr. McNulty, climbs with best of the peloton's mortals. Without Quinn in the early moves of stage fourteen, Healy's bid for glory would have been nipped in the bud. While we are all gob-smacked by the man from Slovenia, the explosion of Sean Quinn's talent in the mountains is also breathtaking.

On Sunday's stage fifteen, I felt like the Emperor Palpatine (that's Darth Vader's boss) when he said, "Ah, everything is proceeding as I have foreseen." I said to a few friends this morning, "it doesn't really matter who goes up the road early and when. Tadej and Jonas and maybe Remco will chase them down, and then Tadej drops Remco, and later, Jonas. And oh, yeah, Alcaraz takes out Djokovic in the Wimbledon men's final." I was not wrong.

Please be aware, this is not the end of the fireworks. Sure, Tadej's lead looks good. 3:09 over Jonas. 5:19 over Remco, but that means nothing to the UAE Team Emirates star. He loves to race his bike. He will continue to attack. He will continue to drop everyone on the climbs. Years ago, US pro Marty Jemison was in a day-long breakaway in the Tour and he just got pipped out of the top three in the small sprint. Said one commentator to Marty, "You must feel terrible. All that work, and you were right there at the end." Said Marty, "It's okay. I had my chance. I thought I could take it. But really, I just like to race my bike." So does Tadej. Except he rarely gets pipped at the line. Well, there was that one time.

Road furniture. It's a fact of modern cycling life because it is a fact of modern life. It makes for safer driving. It makes for much less safe bike racing. When you are in the bunch and not in the first 10-15 guys, you simply cannot see the road furniture until it's too late. The organizers do put padding on some of the furniture, but that doesn't solve the problem of early recognition and avoidance. It just ameliorates the impact and outcome. Here's the solution. It's cheap and easy. Buy a crap-ton of alpine skiing gates or similar product. They are semi-rigid, hollow, around 2 meters in length, and 4.5 cm in diameter. Or since you're going to need a lot, have them manufactured for the all the Grand Tours and make them 3 meters long. Affix a flag to the top. Affix the gate to the top of the lead piece of road furniture. Even from the rear of a strung-out peloton, riders will be able to see the flag and understand that there are dangerous bits of road furniture or a road divider ahead.

Equipment theft. The Tour de France has been in business since 1903. The other Grand Tours, a few years less. You'd think by now they would figure out that the team Service Course vehicles are filled with highly valuable and easily resalable bits of equipment. Perhaps these bikes were even stored in the hotel basement or underground parking lot. I tried to read the article about the theft of eleven TotalEnergies bicycles stolen from their hotel on July 11, but my two years of rarely practiced schoolkid French wasn't enough. You'd think the place would be crawling with security. But Noooooooooooo [said in best John Belushi, Saturday Night Live voice].

Aaron wrote:

Rumors of Jasper's demise were greatly exaggerated. After going the entire first week of the Tour without a stage win and looking ill at ease in attempting to find any success in the early sprint stages, Jasper Philipsen emphatically returned in the second week. In stage ten Alpecin showed off the power of their fully armed and operational battle station. It's likely a 40-something Cat 4 rider could have won the sprint with the ridiculous leadout provided by Mathieu van der Poel, so it was light work for Philipsen to nab his first stage win. Two days later, he'd show another touch of class, emerging from a confusing final few hundred meters to win by over a bike length ahead of Wout van Aert.

Question marks surrounded Philipsen after week one's lack of success, but he answered them emphatically with these two stage wins, even though he couldn't quite make up the ground he'd need to in order to attack the Green Jersey of …

—Biniam Girmay:

Two stages in the first week wasn't enough for Girmay to be satisfied. He continued to display exceptional competitiveness in the *maillot vert* standings through week two, whether by attacking intermediate sprints or with his continued high placements in stage finishes. After coming second to Philipsen in stage ten, he took advantage of the very next sprint finish two days later to earn his third stage win of the year on stage twelve. Girmay has impressed at every opportunity this year, holding on to a firm grasp on the Green Jersey and doing so in style, riding fast, riding fair, and riding with fun.

—Vingegaard's Vindication:

There was an air of manufactured uncertainty around team Visma-Lease a Bike coming into the Tour with the continued questions regarding Jonas Vingegaard's fitness after his devastating crash in the spring, but if he hadn't put them to rest yet by the time the race reached stage eleven, he definitively shut the door on the doubters by winning a two-up sprint over Tadej Pogačar despite the Slovenian's multiple attacks throughout the stage. For Vingegaard, it was vindication against those who thought he might not be ready for the Tour. For Pogačar, it was perhaps a wake-up call—was his feeding timing off? Was he still fighting the demons of the Granon or de la Loze?—and for the viewers, it was hope that this Tour could become a memorably competitive one as the greatest cyclists of this generation battled against the greatest grand tour rider of this generation. One thing was for sure: Vingegaard was not going to be going away easily.

—Pogi at Peak:

Stages fourteen and fifteen would be an entirely different story than stage eleven. Despite the best efforts of Vingegaard and the Visma | Lease a Bike squad, Pogačar was simply better. He and UAE had an answer at every turn, a counter-strategy for everything Visma tried, and when he decided to kick the acceleration up to eleven on Pla d'Adet and Plateau de Beille, no one had any answers for him. UAE, despite (perhaps due to?) the departure of key *domestique* Juan Ayuso, were operating like a well-oiled machine, and their keystone was at its best. Politt and Wellens destroyed the peloton in the low hills, Sivakov, Soler, and Almeida put in turns in the mountains, and trustworthy Adam Yates was there to put their opponents to the screws, launching Pogačar to a 39-second time gain on stage fourteen.

The next day, he put on a simply breathtaking display of climbing skill, marking the fastest time in the history of the Plateau de Beille by nearly 4 minutes. It was a two-day-long hammer blow by Pogačar and his team after which Vingegaard had fallen to a 3-minute deficit on GC with Remco Evenepoel distanced to 5:19. What more can be said about

Pog at this point? He has the *palmares* of an entire career at twenty-five years old, and any time it seems that his opponents have found a weakness, he goes out and forges it into a strength. The final week of this Tour features several incredibly difficult climbing stages, but it's hard to imagine anyone bringing him back to reality after the strength he displayed and the ease with which he distanced all of his rivals on two of the hardest days thus far.

—Remco is for real:

He may be down 5:19 on GC to Pogačar, but Remco Evenepoel has been having himself a very strong debut at the Tour de France. It was expected that he would compete for the podium, to be sure, but the amount of time he has spent right in the wheels with the best climbers in the world on some of the toughest climbs this year will see, in addition to the time he's been able to make up on descents and in the time trial, is impressive beyond compare for the twenty-four-year-old who is still participating in the White Jersey competition, to say nothing of the Yellow. While his chances at winning are slim, he has acquitted himself well, and with a few more Grand Tours under his belt, the sky seems the limit—he will almost assuredly be competing with Pogačar and Vingegaard for years to come.

—Team UAE:

It was mentioned above that Juan Ayuso abandoned the Tour this week, but is it too strange to say that this seems to have benefitted UAE Team Emirates? They seemed better organized, better collected, better strategized over the course of week two despite losing one of their strongest mountain *domestiques*. It re-raises question marks that were discussed as soon as they announced their roster—where was the ever-steady presence of Rafal Majka? where was Brandon McNulty or Mikkel Bjerg?—and while one cannot question team choices that have led to a rider in Yellow and another two inside the top ten, it is interesting to take note of how well UAE conquered the challenges presented by stages fourteen and fifteen despite being down a rider. Time will tell, with week three looming, whether the team will suffer as the kilometers mount, but it's so far so good for UAE in their quest for GC victory and perhaps a sneaky second podium spot to boot.

The Story of the 2024 Tour de France

—Week three: a back-loaded brute:

Lastly, a look ahead. The final week of the 2024 *parcours* is, quite simply, a beast. Stages eighteen, nineteen and twenty are all tremendous challenges, with twelve categorized climbs across them including two HC climbs before the mountaintop finish at Isola 2000 in stage nineteen, and three straight category one climbs throughout stage twenty. The question that we will learn the answer to over the next week is whether or not it'll truly matter. With a 3-minute lead over Jonas Vingegaard, Pogačar and UAE can afford to ride a bit more defensively, controlling the peloton without going for excessive accelerations, and still maintain a comfortable advantage. This would effectively nullify what would otherwise be exciting stages.

However, Tadej is still Tadej; Pog simply loves to ride, loves to accelerate, loves the challenge of competing, so we must look forward to those days regardless of what the time gaps throughout the GC look like, because it is a near-certainty that the most exciting rider in the peloton will continue to look for opportunities to show the world what he's capable of and to put his stamp on this Tour the way he did the Giro.

Chapter 6
Week Three: Time to Climb, and Climb Some More

For the first day back to work the riders would head northeast, from Gruissan to Nîmes, roughly following the Mediterranean coastline, but slightly inland. There was only a single fourth-category climb coming a bit more than half-way through the stage. It looked made for a sprint finish.

The day's real challenge was the weather. At 2:00 PM it was already 33°C (91°F) at the finish city of Nîmes. Plus there were occasional gusts of wind that reached 40 kilometers an hour.

Before the stage start there were two withdrawals triggered by Covid-19 infections, Maxim Van Gils (Lotto Dstny) and Chris Harper (Team Jayco AlUla). That left 150 riders to start the stage. Before the stage's true start the peloton rode along the coast for a few kilometers and upon reaching the resort town of Saint Pierre-la-Mer they turned inland and were given their official start.

Immediately Stefan Küng and Sandy Dujardin took off from the pack. Seeing that no one felt like joining them, they sat up and let the peloton catch them. From there the peloton unambitiously rolled along, going just 37.9 kilometers the first hour.

The pack woke up a bit during the second hour and covered almost 45 kilometers. The day's intermediate sprint came 96 kilometers into the stage with Bryan Coquard winning, beating Jasper Philipsen and Biniam Girmay. But just after the sprint TotalEnergies rider Thomas Gachignard went solo. After roughly 15 kilometers of work as he topped the days only rated climb, the Côte de Fambetou, he had built a 2 minute, 20 second lead.

No one seemed particularly worried about the lone escapee. And indeed without any excitement, with 25 kilometers to go Gachignard was back in the pack.

Once in the finish city of Nîmes the large pack raced down the city's wide streets. With 1.5 kilometers to go there was a crash bringing down Biniam Girmay, Neilson Powless and several other riders. Because they were less than two kilometers from the line they were given the same finishing time as the lead group.

Jasper Philipsen was able to use his superb sprint to win the stage ahead of Phil Bauhaus and Alexander Kristoff. Pogačar finished thirty-seventh, Vingegaard eightieth, both safely buried in the pack. When Pogačar mounted the podium after the stage he received his thirty-fifth Yellow Jersey.

Stage seventeen brought the long-awaited Alpine climbing. But not yet with the full intensity that the formidable mountain range can bring to a stage. The day had three rated ascents, the first being the Col Bayard, a second-category ascent that used to be a regular part of the Tour. From the first time it was part of the Tour in 1905 until its last pre-war inclusion in 1937, the climb was used twenty-three times. Counting 2024, the Col Bayard has been used just four times since.

The days' next mountain has nothing like the Col Bayard's history. The 7.5 kilometer, first category Col du Noyer was being used in the Tour for only the fifth time, the first time being stage thirteen of the 1970 Tour. The stage finished with the third-category climb to the Superdévoluy Ski Station.

Early on the peloton was thinned. Phil Bauhaus and Elmar Reinders did not start, Reinders going home for the birth of his first child. About 50 kilometers into the stage and clearly suffering, Alexei Lutsenko abandoned. Then Fernando Gaviria (Movistar) and Sam Bennett (Decathlon Ag2r) quit the race.

Though attacks did not go off at the gun, the day was filled with aggression. About 9 kilometers into the stage several Visma | Lease a Bike riders tried to scoot away, but that didn't work. A little later on there was a split in the peloton and UAE Team Emirates riders Adam Yates, Marc Soler and Pavel Sivakov found themselves on the wrong side of the fracture.

The peloton re-grouped about 17 kilometers into the stage, triggering attacks and counter-attacks. Even a break of Wout van Aert, Tobias Halland Johannessen, Jarrad Drizners and Harold Tejada could only stay away for 6 kilometers.

Triggered by an attack by Magnus Cort, a break of four was formed when he was joined by Tiesj Benoot, Bob Jungels and Romain Gregoire at about kilometer 57. The peloton was not pleased with this development and the chase was hard. But come the intermediate sprint at kilometer 115, Cort was the first of the break across the line with the chasing peloton just 45 seconds back.

Five kilometers later a group of forty-seven riders broke clear of the peloton, which signaled its acquiescence to the move by letting them go. Come the Col Bayard at kilometer 146 the front quartet was 1 minute, 45 seconds ahead of the big break and 4 minutes, 50 seconds ahead of the peloton, being led by UAE Team Emirates. At the top of the Col Bayard the quartet was 30 seconds ahead of a pair of riders who had left the big break behind, Guillaume Martin and Valentin Madouas. The remains of the big break were 1 minute behind the front four. The pack with the GC riders was now 6 minutes, 40 seconds behind the leaders.

At the foot of the first-category Col du Noyer, Martin and Madouas made contact with the front four, with the chasing group 40 seconds back. From the chasing group Simon Yates attacked. He caught and dropped the front break. Richard Carapaz also bolted from the chasing group and quickly caught Yates while they were climbing the Col du Noyer.

Carapaz dropped Yates 1.8 kilometers from the summit and took off in search of a stage win at the top of the Superdévoluy climb.

He did it, crossing the finish line 37 seconds ahead of Yates. The GC contenders started coming in about 7 minutes after Carapaz's finish, with Pogačar 10 seconds behind Evenepoel and Vingegaard just 2 seconds behind the Yellow Jersey.

The day's difficulty was made clear when about 20 minutes after Carapaz finished only 81 of the day's 145 finishers had arrived. It would be more than twenty minutes before the rest of the pack came home.

After the stage Carapaz said, "This victory means everything! I've been trying to get it since the start of the Tour; that was the goal. In the general classification we are very far away, but the hope remained of winning a stage.

"It was a very difficult day, with a lot of attacks, but in the end, a large group formed. I was able to come out at the right time and I managed to get this result which I will remember forever. I really made the most of the moment. I knew the final well having studied it with my sports director."

After stage seventeen's monster climbs, stage eighteen was a series of five third-category climbs with an unrated uphill trip to the finish. There was nary a flat meter to be found on the route. A day like this screamed for a break.

The peloton agreed with this assessment with attacks flying off at the start. Among the aggressive riders trying to get away was world champion Mathieu van der Poel. Despite his efforts, he was not a part of the twenty riders who got clear at kilometer 26, just before the first climb. But with continued aggression, a total of thirty-seven riders did escape.

Michael Matthews won the intermediate sprint that was 84.3 kilometers into the stage. At this point the big break had a lead of 5 minutes, 40 seconds. On the Côte de Saint-Apollinaire, the fourth of the day's five climbs, the leaders went over the top 10 minutes, 30 seconds ahead of the bunch.

On the day's final categorized climb, the Côte des Demoiselles Coiffées, 35 kilometers from the finish, Michal Kwiatkowski went over the top first and on the descent he was joined by Mattéo Vercher and Victor Campenaerts.

Over the remaining 25 kilometers of undulating road the trio worked well together building a small, but sustainable gap. With 15 kilometers to go they had a 40-second lead on five chasers that included Jai Hindley.

The trio made it safely to the finish with speedy Campenaerts taking the stage, and Vercher and Kwiatkowski coming in second and third. The Yellow Jersey group with Vingegaard and Evenepoel came in 13 minutes, 40 seconds later.

After the stage an ecstatic Victor Campenaerts said, "A true pro must ride the Tour de France, finish the Tour de France, and win a stage in the Tour de France. That is everyone's dream, and now, here in Barcelonnette, I can make it come true. It's unbelievable. I've had the full support of my team over the past weeks. I went on a nine-week high-altitude training camp to prepare. All that time, my girlfriend, heavily pregnant, was by my side. While the rest of the team prepared for this Tour in the Dauphiné or the Tour of Switzerland, we were in the hospital in Spain for the birth of our son. That week was supposed to be a heavy training week for me. 'See what you can do,' my coach said. But I was tireless. Since Gustaaf was born, I've been riding on clouds."

The Story of the 2024 Tour de France

On Friday the nineteenth, the Tour sent the riders into nose-bleed territory with three monster climbs, the first two *Hors Catégorie* followed by a first-category hilltop finish.

Tour boss Christian Prudhomme wrote this about the stage, "The menu for this ultra-mountain stage could well make you dizzy, but it'll also whet the appetite of the very best climbers. Although the stage is less than 150 kilometers long, the riders will climb above 2,000 meters on three occasions, the biggest test is the climb to the summit of La Bonette, the highest road in France at an altitude of 2,802 meters."

The first mountain was the Col de Vars and this would be the thirty-sixth time the mountain has been included in the Tour, starting in 1922 when Belgian Philippe Thys was first to its summit. Coming from the north, the riders would face 18.8 kilometers averaging 5.7 percent. But that isn't the entire story. Early in the climb there are sections as steep as 10.5 percent. Getting over this monster would be a hard way to spend part of a July afternoon.

Then, cresting 87.5 kilometers into the stage, The Cime de la Bonette was 22.9 kilometers averaging 6.6 percent. It is a fairly steady climb with a sting in its tail. The final kilometers average 10.3 percent. The big climb hasn't been used very often in the Tour. Riders were sent up it for the first time in stage eighteen of the 1962 Tour when legendary climber (and winner of the 1962 Tour) Federico Bahamontes was first over the mountain. This would be only the fifth time the Cime de la Bonette has been used in the Tour.

The riders would finish the day with the 16.1 kilometer climb to the Isola 2000 ski station. The 16.1 kilometer climb averages 7.1 percent with the first two kilometers rising at ten and more percent.

Early on twenty-two riders got clear and at the intermediate sprint at Guillestre, 21 kilometers into the stage, Bryan Coquard was first over the line. Come the Col du Vars, the breakaway started falling apart. Leaving the peloton, Richard Carapaz and Simon Yates bridged up to the front riders. Olympic champion Carapaz was first over the Col du Vars ahead of Matteo Jorgenson, Wilko Kelderman and Ilan Van Wilder and five other survivors of the break. The peloton was chasing at 3 minutes, 30 seconds back.

By the time the break reached the first slopes of the Cime de la Bonette the gap had grown to 4 minutes, 30 seconds. Carapaz was again first over the summit. That was enough to make him the owner of the Polka-Dot Jersey when he rode into the Isola 2000 ski station at the end of the stage.

Approaching the final climb the break was down to five riders: Richard Carapaz, Matteo Jorgenson, Simon Yates, Jai Hindley and Wilco Kelderman. First off the back of the break was Hindley. A few meters after Hindley was detached Jorgenson attacked and was quickly alone and off the front.

Back in the front group of chasers, Pogačar attacked with 9.5 kilometers to go. Evenepoel and Vingegaard tried to stay with the flying Slovenian, but he would not be contained. Two kilometers into his attack he was 20 seconds ahead of his two main rivals. Pogačar passed Jorgenson 1.9 kilometers from the summit and headed to the finish for another solo stage win, bowing to the crowd as he crossed the line. Jorgenson followed in 21 seconds later with Simon Yates third, finishing 40 seconds after Pogačar. Then Carapaz, Evenpoel and Vingegaard came in.

After the stage Pogačar said, "Now I can confirm that La Bonette is a very scary climb to race. At least in training you can skip the final kilometer! I'm super happy I had good legs today. We trained here the whole month between the Giro and the Tour. It was a very hard training camp with no easy days, as we had to climb every day.

"My teammates and I have talked already of how badly we wanted to race this day, and we raced as we said, setting everything up to the point when I attacked. It was perfect. I was a little bit empty in the final two kilometers of the stage. When I caught Carapaz and Simon Yates, I felt I was already on my limit. Then I saw Matteo and pushed through to overtake him at great speed. That killed my legs and I was afraid that he might come back to outsprint me. He was very strong today, as was the rest of the breakaway. Chapeau to all of them."

Pogačar was now 5 minutes, 3 seconds ahead of Vingegaard and 7 minutes, 1 second ahead of Evenepoel. He had tossed and gored the finest stage racers in the world with ease. It was an incredible performance.

Back into the mountains. There would be no letup in the 2024 Tour's penultimate stage, a trip from Nice on the coast, north into the Alpes-de-Haute-Provence. The riders faced four highly rated ascents, including a hilltop stage finish.

The Story of the 2024 Tour de France

First off, the riders would be sent over the Col de Braus. This would be the twenty-eighth time since 1911 (though only the third time since the war) that Tour riders had been sent over this 10-kilometer, second-category ascent averaging 6.6%.

Sixty kilometers into the stage came the first-category 20.7 kilometer Col de Turini. Though it averages 5.7 percent, there are lengthy chunks of 6.6 to 8 percent gradient. The Turini was seeing only its fifth inclusion on the Tour, the first coming in 1948 when Louison Bobet, the first man to win the Tour three years in a row (1953–55), was first over the mountain.

Thirty-six kilometers later the riders would encounter the first-category Col de la Colmiane, also called the Col Saint-Martin. This one was steeper, 7.5 kilometers averaging 7.1 percent. The Tour has only used it only four times, the first in 1973.

Most famously the ascent was part of 1975 Tour de France's fifteenth stage. Eddy Merckx had been punched in the liver by a spectator during the fourteenth stage. This undoubtedly weakened the Belgian. In stage fifteen he was overcome by weakness and Bernard Thévenet steamed right by him to win the stage and go on to win that Tour. Eddy Merckx never again won the Tour de France.

The mountain remained unused until 2020 when it was the first climb of the twelfth stage which saw French racer Benoît Cosnefroy first over the mountain.

For a punishing finish to the stage, the riders would cross the line atop the Col de la Couillole after climbing 15.7 kilometers of 7.1% gradient. Though the Tour has climbed this pass twice before, in 1973 and 1975, this was the first time it had been used as a stage finish.

GC third-place Remco Evenepoel announced in advance that since his goal to win the final time trial the next day, he did not intend to go deep on this stage.

In the opening kilometers teams Uno-X and EF Education-Easy-Post tried to form an escape group, to no avail. As the pack approached the first climb, the Col de Braus, a break with several GC top-ten riders formed. That brought about an immediate reaction from the GC top three and their teammates that closed the gap.

Then two of the 2024 Tour's more aggressive riders, Wilco Kelderman and Bruno Armirail escaped from the re-grouped peloton. This move stirred no reaction from the pack. Soon Enric Mas bridged up to the pair. An unworried Yellow Jersey group followed at 55 seconds.

Mas led Kelderman and Armirail over the Col de Bras and on the descent Jan Tratnik, Marc Soler, Richard Carapaz, Clement Champoussin and Romain Bardet formed a group to chase the trio.

Come the Col de Turini the lead trio was 35 seconds ahead of the Tratnik chase group and 2 minutes ahead of the pack, which had grown with a regrouping in the kilometers leading to the mountain. Once on the climb the Tratnik group, less Champoussin, caught the leaders 9 kilometers from the summit. One kilometer from the top Kevin Geniets, Tobias Johannessen and Jasper Stuyven bridged the gap up to the front group, making it ten riders off the front.

Jasper Stuyven won the intermediate sprint that came 87.8 kilometers into the stage with the peloton now 3 minutes, 50 seconds behind the break.

Richard Carapaz had been first over the Turini and come the Col de la Colmiane, Carapaz was again first man over the top. That gave him an unassailable lead in the climber classification. There were not enough climber's points left in the 2024 Tour to take it away from him. If he finished the Tour he would go home with the Polka-Dot Jersey.

There was still one more climb to get over this day, the first-category Col de la Couillole. The leaders reached the base of the mountain 2 minutes, 45 seconds ahead of the pack. But once the road started to rise the break fell apart. About 11.4 kilometers from the finish Enric Mas and Richard Carapaz attacked. Briefly Romain Bardet was able to stay with them, but he was quickly shucked and the pair were gone.

Back down the hill with 5 kilometers to go Vingegaard attacked from the reduced GC group and immediately had Pogačar on his tail. Evenepoel tried but could not stay with the pair. Pogačar and Vingegaard caught the lead duo, but Mas was unable to match their speed and then Carapaz was also dropped.

And close to the top Pogačar went clear to win the stage 7 seconds ahead of Vingegaard. Carapaz finished 23 seconds after Pogačar and Evenepoel crossed the line 53 seconds after the unstoppable Yellow Jersey.

After the stage Vingegaard reflected on the day's efforts, "It was a tough and hot day. I felt better today than yesterday. Then I had one of my worst days ever. I felt good when Remco attacked. I thought to myself that now it was my time. I rode after that mainly to secure second place. Remco is the best time trialist in the world, so it's definitely not over yet. I'm glad I was able to take almost a minute today."

"Tadej was [on my wheel] a little more today. I think I would have done the same thing if I were in his shoes. I'm happy with how I rode today, and that I was able to recover from the lesser days. To bounce back this way, that makes me feel fulfilled. The legs were really much better. I rode around all day with confidence. Tomorrow I will give everything again in the final time trial."

There was just one stage left, the 33.7 kilometer individual time trial with both the second-category La Turbie climb 11 kilometers into the stage and the unrated Col d'Eze 6 kilometers later. It would start in Monaco and wind its way through switchbacks and tight curves along the coast to finish in Nice. In Nice they would be on the coastal road, heading out the famed Promenade des Anglais, then do a 180 and after a short distance take a left inland for an arrival at the end of the 2024 Tour de France at Nice's main square, the Place Masséna.

In advance of the stage Tour boss Christian Prudhomme wrote, "Everyone remembers the last occasion the Tour finished with a time trial, when Greg LeMond stripped the Yellow Jersey from the shoulders of Laurent Fignon on the Champs-Élysées in 1989, by just 8 seconds. Thirty-five years on, we can but dream of a similar duel, involving two or three riders, an authentic athletic confrontation whose outcome would determine the final podium of the 111th edition, and the first to finish far from its familiar Parisian setting, the ultimate finale destined for Place Masséna, just a few pedal-strokes from the Promenade des Anglais."

But the circumstances were hardly the same. LeMond was just 50 seconds behind Fignon before that famous time trial. We know now that was a bridgeable gap. But in 2024 the GC difference between Pogačar and Vingegaard was 5 minutes, 14 seconds. Only the most extraordinary catastrophe would keep Pogačar from winning the Tour at this point.

There were 141 riders left in the Tour to ride the final stage. Astana Qazaqstan rider Davide Ballerini was first off, followed by Mark Cavendish in the final Tour de France stage of his career.

The final three riders were Evenepoel, Vingegaard and Pogačar. Pogačar turned in a stunning ride, beating Vingegaard by 1 minute, 3 seconds. Evenepoel, a very capable time trialist who had hoped to win this stage was 1 minute, 14 seconds slower than the Slovenian. Pogačar seemed unbothered by the two climbs, and blasted down the Col d'Eze at 91.2 kilometers an hour.

That gave him six stage wins and the final Yellow Jersey. Extraordinary. One has to reach back to 1979 when Bernard Hinault won his second Tour to find an equivalent domination.

Final General Classification, after 3,498 kilometers raced at an average speed of 41.818 kilometers/hour:

1. Tadej Pogačar: 83 hours, 38 minutes, 56 seconds
2. Jonas Vingegaard @ 6 minutes, 17 seconds
3. Remco Evenepoel @ 9 minutes, 18 seconds
4. Joao Almeida @ 19 minutes, 3 seconds
5. Mikel Landa @ 20 minutes, 6 seconds

Richard Carapaz won the Mountains Classification while Biniam Girmay won the Points Classification. Remco Evenepoel was the Best Young Rider and UAE Team Emirates was the Teams Classification winner.

Before we leave the 2024 Tour de France, here's a final look at the race from David and Aaron Stanley:

Here are David's thoughts:

There are many ways to rule the peloton of the Tour de France as patron. If you are Bernard Hinault, you rule with threats of physical intimidation. As Jacques Anquetil, you rule with a sense of grandeur and the air of an emperor. But just as no one expects the Spanish Inquisition—whose diverse weapons are fear, surprise, ruthless efficiency, an almost fanatical devotion to the Pope, and nice red uniforms—no one expects a patron whose good sportsmanship and 'aw, shucks' attitude are wrapped around one of the greatest aerobic engines ever seen on two wheels, and an assassin's heart that beats with icy cold. Tadej Pogačar, the UAE Team Emirates leader, is the patron we didn't know we needed.

This has been a stunning Tour. Not all Tours are memorable. Think back to 2019. Egan Bernal wins, the first Latin American winner, and the youngest winner since 1909. But what do we remember? Hailstorms and landslides. Yet this Tour has been marked by a detonation of greatness. Fifteen things (alphabetically) I'll remember.

The Story of the 2024 Tour de France

1. Asshats. See also: social media. People are jealous asshats. When Tadej went on the attack in stage nineteen, caught, and passed Matteo Jorgenson, I saw an explosion of social media hate that reminded me why sports fans can be incredible jerks. When Michael Jordan and the Chicago Bulls and the '60s-era Boston Celtics were winning everything, people hated them. No one outside of Manchester ever loved Man U at their peak. Jack Nicklaus was despised for taking down the people's choice, Arnie Palmer. Same with the New England Patriots and Tom Brady. A friend of Italian heritage told me of how his Italian grandfather used to seethe—how *Nonno* hated Eddy Merckx. Eddy, you might recall, won a lot of races and was not known for gifting stages to anyone.

Let's have Neal Rogers, ex-editor of *Velo-News*, put this into perspective. "Mark Cavendish breaking the record for all-time Tour de France stage wins: Marvelous, fantastic, sublime, heroic, historic. Tadej Pogačar winning [six] stages en route to a third Tour de France victory: Questionable, dishonorable, arrogant, short-sighted, greedy. Make that make sense."

Reddit, Threads, Twitter, FB—all over the sport-i-verse cycling fans were screaming about how Tadej had ruined the Tour, how he wasn't sporting, how he was a selfish jerk. That, of course, is grotesque bullshit. First off, Tadej is a highly paid professional. He is paid to win races and get his sponsors as much face time as possible with the world. He is not paid to gift other riders stage wins. We don't see this "gifting wins" in any other world sport. Hell, most of you probably don't let your kids win at Monopoly or ping-pong. Did any of Sepp Kuss's teammates gift him anything at the 2023 Vuelta? Who the hell wants a gift, anyway? *Pas de cadeaux*, mates. *Pas de cadeaux.*

2. Cheating. Is something going on? Maybe. We've all seen this before and we've earned the right to our skepticism. The cheating drumbeats were loud when Tadej, and several others, all raced the Plateau de Beille at record speeds and destroyed Marco Pantani's 26-year-old record. We all know that Pantani was doped with enough EPO to treat an entire cancer ward's worth of chemo-induced anemia, but does that mean so were Tadej and his flying cohorts?

No, it does not. There are plenty of scholarly pieces out there that detail the mechanical advantages twenty-six years of technological advances have given today's peloton. I've ridden dozens of race bikes since I started racing in 1979. A 2024 pro bike is as far removed from Pantani's 1998 bike as my first real race bike, a 1979 CCM Tour de Canada, was from the bike ridden by Louison Bobet when he won the 1953 Tour de France. According to a site that measures rolling resistance, a modern, tubeless race tire is 9–12 watts more efficient than the race tires of 1998. That doesn't include the aero advantage of the tire/rim interface, the aero advantage of the modern wheel, the ceramic bearings, the airflow between wheel and fork blades, the energy retained due to the stiffness of the rim-spoke-hub combination, but simply the improvements in treads and materials which decrease the rolling resistance dramatically. Another site crunched the numbers and determined that a modern wheel, in total, is anywhere from 35–50 watts more efficient than Pantani's.

What else is markedly more efficient? The modern frame and cockpit. Chains and chain lubes. Oversized pulleys. Chainring and pedal and shoe and clothing and helmet aerodynamics. Electronic shifting—you no longer scrub off speed as the chain clicks into location as it does with human shifting. Don't forget, Tadej is a far more aerodynamic rider than Marco. Pantani, to quote Paul Sherwen (we miss you, Paul) is "all over his machine!" He had terrible form, always in and out of the saddle, bouncing around, and he created an immense amount of human drag. Tadej, (again to quote Paul), "is locked into his machine."

These are not marginal gains like bringing your own pillow from home. These gains are measurable and significant. If scandal does break out, and we learn that hijinks are afoot at the Team UAE Emirates bus, I promise to be the first to admit I was wrong. While we pile on the UAE lads, let's step back and note that if UAE are up to something, so are the fellows from Visma | Lease a Bike. Consider this stat from Orla on The Breakaway, which was shared to me from the kind people at Write-Bike-Repeat:

> Orla on the Breakaway, regarding the rivalry between Tadej and Jonas: in four TOUR DE FRANCEs—84 stages—their accumulated time is separated by just 1:25.

Four Tours. Roughly 82 hours each. A total of 328 hours of racing. Just 85 seconds separate these two young men.

You won't let it go? The lack of physical evidence is noteworthy. As I said, if I'm wrong, you'll read my *mea culpa* here. Boy howdy, I hope I'm right.

3. Richard Carapaz. Polka Dots suit him. The Ecuadorian is the definitive plucky rider. With an impressive *palmares*, he is the first cyclist to achieve an Olympic road race gold medal and a podium finish in each of the three Grand Tours. He ignites every race with serious climbs afoot. He took the Yellow Jersey after stage three, and became the first Ecuadorian rider to do so. He went on to win stage seventeen, as he crossed the finish more than 7 minutes before Pogačar, who took back the *maillot jaune* after stage four. By winning his stage, he became the first Ecuadorian to win a stage at each of the Grand Tours. Simply, he races with passion and grinta and exuberance. He's fun to watch.

4. Mark Cavendish. He didn't quit. With Tour-stage-win number thirty-five in his musette, it would've been easy for him to bail during the brutality of several mountain stages. But he did not. He brings honor to himself and to his thirty-five Tour wins and his total of 165 professional victories with his combativeness. You saw him on Saturday, in the last few kilometers of his last road stage in his last Tour de France, the fourteenth Tour in his career? Waving, smiling, soaking it in. Then, as he crossed the line, he broke into tears into the arms of his teammates. The thirty-nine-year-old Cav is, as he has always claimed, "a really good bike racer."

5. Biniam Girmay. Green, even Skoda green, looks good on him. As I wrote last week, he is an extraordinary national hero. Bigger than Lionel Messi in Argentina, bigger than peak Tiger Woods here in the States. His feats in this year's Tour will inspire an entire generation of young people in Eritrea for the next ten years. If I ran a pro squad, I'd put together a load of bikes, a bunch of coaches, and travel through the Horn of Africa in search of thirty teens whose parents are willing to move with their children to Europe to live, school, and train. Out of that group, I am convinced, would come the first great generation of Black African cyclists and certainly the first Black African Grand Tour champions. Biniam said that when he saw Daniel Teklehaimanot take the Polka-Dot Jersey very early on in the Tour back in 2015, it showed him he could do it too.

6. Ben Healy. I love Ben; unabashedly and openly. His aggression and combativity were second to no one in this year's Tour. He was always

on the attack, and in a year with a lesser version of Tadej, he might well have won his stage.

7. Matteo Jorgenson. I love this guy, too. I was gutted for him when Tadej blew past him with just a wee bit to go. But truly, didn't everyone, including Matteo as he neared the top of stage nineteen, realize that he would most certainly get caught by the soaring Pogačar? Matteo, with a skidding crash, still earned a fourth place finish in the final time trial, 2minutes, 8 seconds behind Tadej. He finished the Tour in eighth place on GC, only 26 minutes, 34 seconds behind the Yellow Jersey. A remarkable accomplishment for the twenty-five-year-old from Walnut Creek.

Matteo showed the world that while his Visma | Lease a Bike team leader Jonas Vingegaard perhaps missed Sepp Kuss (the 2023 Vuelta winner out with Covid), he was no slouch, and clearly equally adept at working for JV. He was more than an outstanding teammate on the road. He was a true teammate on the team bus, too. Said Matteo to JV after the heartbreak of stage nineteen to Isola 2000, where Jonas conceded he could not beat Tadej. "Hey, I'm proud of you," Jorgenson said. "You gave everything, that's all that matters, really." That's a stand-up guy you want on your team. Kudos, MJ, man. Kudos.

8. The Pentagon of Cycling. Learned cycling folks spoke of how it was nearly impossible, in the twenty-first century, for a rider to do the Giro–Tour double. They were right for twenty-three years. I propose a new standard; the Pentagon of Cycling. Is it possible for a rider to win the Giro, Tour de France, Olympics, Vuelta, and the Worlds? In a single year? Probably not. In a career, quite possibly. But in 2024, don't say impossible.

9. Matthieu van der Poel. Remember back in my preview piece when I said that Astana had hired the world's best lead-out man, Michael Morkov, to lead Cav to the promised land of thirty-five stage wins? Yeah, I was all kinds of wrong. Morkov is terrific, but it's really MvdP who owns the title of the world's greatest lead-out man these days. What he did for teammate Jasper Philipsen as JP took three stage wins on stages ten, thirteen, and sixteen was exceptional. It was clear to me that MvdP was using this race to build for the Paris Games and I'll be shocked, yes shocked, if MvdP doesn't stand on the top step of the Paris podium. His

power, fitness, and race-reading ability are a step above the rest of the world in a one day hilly race. [Ed: Remco Evenepoel won the Olympic road race and time trial]

10. Nils Pollitt. Joseph Bruyère was the super lieutenant of Eddy Merckx. Indurain was the power behind the greatness of Delgado. Sean Yates. Tim Wellens. Tim Declercq. Every great team has a guy who can sit on the front at 45–50 kph for ten minutes, roll off for 1 minute, and then go back to the front, and repeat the cycle for 100 km. UAE Team Emirates' Nils Pollitt is that guy. For this race, we've also seen the 1.9 meters, 81-kg guy go up the hills well, too. An immensely strong *rouleur* with a solid *palmares* in the cobbled, one day classics, the thirty-year-old German is simply indomitable.

11. Christian Prudhomme. The Tour, you might know, has two starts. The first is the roll-out, known as the *départ fictif*. It's a neutral zone, no riders may pass the lead vehicle, which is generally run at thirty or so kilometers per hour, and runs for several kilometers from the *village départ* until out of town. It is a start parade. Outside of town, the actual start, the *départ réel* takes place. At that moment, early every afternoon, race director Christian Prudhomme rose up from the vehicle through the sunroof to wave a flag like a sunflower growing up into the breeze. As the sunflower Prudhomme unfurled its leaves, the stage was on.

12. Race Radio. The UCI will run several major races later this summer without team-car/rider radios. Whether that will affect the Tour in 2025 or beyond is yet to be told. But I speak of the race radios today. We can now listen to the comms between team directors and the riders. Some are broadcast on air. Some are broadcast on the Tour's official website. At first, it seems quite cool, to peel back that curtain. Then you realize, to listen into the radios is to listen in to workplace talk everywhere. "Hey, can I get a bottle and gel?" "I need to get rid of these gilets, guys." "Hey, fellas, the road narrows, get to the front, okay?" "Okay, guys, we gotta be at the front here. Keep protecting 'Star Rider' and let's get someone in the break early." Plus, the inevitable workplace bitching about a colleague–"Jeezus, where the f*** is Wolfgang? Get his ass up here to take a couple pulls. I been on the front the last 8k. F***, where is that asshole?"

13. Remco. Youngest man to win stages in all three Grand Tours. A kid with a sense of humor. A kid not afraid to offer an opinion: "He has no balls" in the heat of battle. A kid not afraid to give props to another rider and reach out with a fist bump. Also, a kid who can crush the GC and the time trials. He's really, really good, and fun to watch. As this bit is written on Saturday as I watch stage twenty, I think he takes the Sunday time trial. I hear it's nice in Nice this time of year. (He didn't win the TT. Whoops-a-daisy.)

14. Unsung Hero. Kudos and chapeau! to Davide (no relation to Classics great Franco) Ballerini. The Astana man has several major wins to his *palmares*. A professional since 2017, he has won the 2021 Het Nieuwsblad, the 2022 Coppa Bernocchi and a gold medal in the road race in the 2019 European Games. But for this race, he had one job, and one job only—make 100% certain that Mark Cavendish survived the toughest days in the mountains so that Cav was able to start the closing time trial on stage twenty-one. A lot of work went into Astana's Project 35 and I feel comfortable saying that without Ballerini's selflessness, the odds of the Tour's Stage Winning Champion seeing the finish drop down to about 20%.

15. Jonas Vingegaard. A hundred days ago Vingegaard's life changed. A terrible crash at the Tour of the Basque Country left the Dane with a broken collarbone, fractured ribs, a fractured scapula, and a collapsed lung. It's terrifying. As he lay in the ICU, pumps running and tubes everywhere in his body, he felt he might well die. There are few worse feelings. In 2012, I was admitted to the ICU with fourteen blood clots in my lungs, any one of which might break free, travel to my heart, and kill me. I was scared to go to sleep because I thought I might not wake up. Jonas, just 100 days ago, was in a similar state. He checked out of hospital on April 16, and on July 21st, he stood on the second step of the podium in the world's most grueling athletic event. That is the equal of Tadej's majesty as he claims the Giro–Tour double.

Yes, the equal. In sport, wins matter. In life, wins look different.

Vive le France! Vive le Tour! Vive les Jeux Olympiques!

Aaron wrote:

This year's Tour de France had drama, monotony, excitement, joy, heartbreak—in short, just another edition of the most important race on the cycling calendar. Here are a few thoughts on some of my favorite storylines of the 2024 iteration of *la grande boucle*.

—The Green Jersey Fight

It was hard to decide, going into the Tour this year, what the battle for the Green Jersey might end up looking like, but it feels safe to say that virtually no one anticipated the eventual outcome. Jasper Philipsen seemed the overwhelming favorite as the fastest man with the best team around him; Arnaud de Lie came to the Tour fresh off winning the Belgian nationals with an explosive finish; Mads Pedersen and Dylan Groenewegen were poised as ever to fight for stage wins; Mark Cavendish was once more seeking his white whale, the thirty-fifth stage win of his career.

Who, then, expected it to be Eritrea's Biniam Girmay who would take the race by storm? He became the first Black African to win a stage and wear the Green Jersey, and he and his Intermarché-Wanty team saw no reason to give it up easily. The battle that ensued between Girmay and Philipsen across intermediate sprints and stage finishes alike was a fierce one, and while Philipsen certainly got his, finishing with three wins, Girmay would be the ultimate victor, winning three stages of his own and wearing the Green Jersey into Nice. This was a true ascension for Girmay, and it was clear throughout the Tour how much it meant for him, his team, and everyone back in his hometown of Asmara. It is not every year we the viewers are privy to such feel-good stories, but Girmay's triumph—to say nothing of Cavendish finally reaching the elusive milestone of the stage-wins record—was an easy storyline to root for with an eventual satisfying ending.

—EF Education First

Possibly the most exciting squad to follow over the course of the race, EF had their share of ups and downs throughout the race, lowlighted by an inability to contest sprint finishes with Marijn van den Berg. Nonetheless, the team earned a day in Yellow in week one, with Richard Carapaz pulling on the *maillot jaune* after stage three based on sum of placements.

Though Neilson Powless suffered a broken bone in his wrist during stage twelve, he fought onward all the same, remaining in the race and putting forth effort at the front of the peloton day in and day out. Ben Healy and Carapaz spent countless hours in breakaways on mountain days; they toiled away, in Dan Jenkins' words, like dogged victims of inexorable fate, doomed to watch the likes of Pogačar, Vingegaard, and Evenepoel motor past them at 7.5 watts/kilogram up the slopes of the highest mountains, saying "good effort lads, we'll take it from here" as they swept up the stage wins.

Finally, though, stage seventeen brought triumph to the men in pink. With Charles Wegelius surely in his ear urging "cam on Richie, cam on", Carapaz dropped Simon Yates and Stevie Williams from an elite group of six to claim the first Tour stage win of his career atop the Superdévoluy. For EF, it was the culmination of several weeks of valiant but theretofore unsuccessful efforts, their hard work paying off after days upon days spent in breakaways or working to put their sprint train at the head of the peloton on the flat days. Carapaz would venture forth and take the Polka-Dot Jersey the day after, and thanks to his efforts throughout the last ten days of the Tour was additionally awarded the supercombativity prize. Despite their early uncertainty, EF were a team that placed the spotlight upon themselves through sheer force of will over the course of the three weeks of the Tour, and they deserve a great deal of credit for everything their racers put themselves through in pursuit of success in any form.

—Victor Campenaerts and the Emotions of the Tour

In 2023, Matej Mohoric won stage nineteen and won the hearts of fans everywhere with his tearful, heartfelt interview where he expressed the difficulty and cruelty of cycling. In 2024, it was Victor Campenaerts, after winning stage eighteen, who provided another emotional moment at the Tour, sharing his struggles with contract talks with his Lotto-Dstny team, his altitude training camp prior to the race, and all of the support his extremely pregnant wife lent him in the lead-up to the Tour de France. It was a poignant moment for the Belgian rider who put himself through so much and put so much pressure on himself and finally earned the greatest reward imaginable, and it was a touching reminder of the humanity present in the peloton.

The Story of the 2024 Tour de France

Cyclists may appear at times like machines, built to push watts for endless hours and repeat for weeks, months, years on end, but hearing from riders such as Mohoric and Campenaerts reminds us all of what is given up to become a professional in one of the most demanding sports on the planet and all that is required from teammates, friends, and family to reach the highest levels of success.

—Pogačar: GOAT in the making?

Tadej Pogačar has a career's *palmares* through five months of racing in 2024 alone. He won Strade Bianche by 2 minutes, 44 seconds; the Volta a Catalunya by 3 minutes, 41 seconds; Liege–Bastogne–Liege by 1 minute, 39 seconds. At the Giro d'Italia, he won six stages and wore the *maglia rosa* for twenty of twenty-one days en route to a 9 minute, 56 second margin of victory and the mountains classification to boot. The Tour de France, though, was his greatest triumph. Despite a gigantic target on his back and challengers including Jonas Vingegaard and Remco Evenepoel gunning for him at every turn, Pogačar put on a performance that can only be described as supernatural. He won six stages, taking his total to twelve in two Grand Tours of the year, including the final three in a row, becoming the first non-sprinter in nearly ninety years to win three consecutive Tour de France stages. He beat back all comers, no matter what was thrown his way. He dominated the race with panache, shining resplendently in the *maillot jaune* for nineteen days. (For those playing along at home, that means Pog spent thirty-nine out of forty-two days across the first two Grand Tours wearing the leader's jersey. As one does.)

There are those who say dominance of this level is boring. But Pogačar makes himself impossible to dislike. He takes such obvious joy in cycling, in competing, in the thrill of the race; he has a smile, a joke, a handshake for anyone he finds himself next to in the peloton. Stylistically, he is a joy to watch, winning with a true sense of style, attacking even when there's no reason to do so, nothing to be gained, simply to push his legs, to have some fun. The only question left to answer for Pogačar, at merely twenty-five years old, is how many records can he set? He holds three Tour wins and seventeen stages, a Giro win with six stages, twelve other stage race wins, and six monuments. Again, at twenty-five years old. The sky seems the limit, and it will surely be thrilling to watch him the rest of the way in 2024 as he chases the Olympics and Worlds and beyond into the future. What heights can cycling reach? Pogačar may be the one to teach us.

—The route

This year's *parcours* came to mixed reviews: there were quite a few unfortunately dull flat days, a polarizing gravel stage, and a range of high mountain stages that were difficult to predict—were some too early, others too late? Would the mountaintop finishes provide the drama we've come to expect? In the end, this Tour's route receives high marks for the latter two, but low marks for the former. Thanks largely to the tireless efforts of Jonas Abrahamsen, the flat stages managed to have at least some intrigue, but for the most part the control levied upon the peloton by the GC teams prevented breakaways from having any success, and while a solution to this issue will be difficult to discover, it's an area of the race that requires continued work. On the other hand, stage nine exceeded expectations, providing one of the most exciting and dramatic stages of the entire Tour, and there were countless highlights in the mountain stages; all told, one can consider the race design as a whole largely successful.

—The teams: some quick thoughts

Finishing at the top of the team standings, UAE got everything they came for, with Pogi winning six stages and the GC, Almeida finishing in fourth, and Adam Yates in sixth. Juan Ayuso was their lone lowlight in frankly confusing fashion, but otherwise it is virtually impossible to find fault with UAE this year. Visma | Lease a Bike had impossible standards to live up to after their ridiculous 2023 season, but Jonas Vingegaard pushed the limits of recovery from injury to finish second overall and win a stage while Matteo Jorgenson raced his way to an eighth-place finish. Detractors will consider this an unsuccessful Tour, especially given the underperformance of Wout van Aert, but Visma | Lease a Bike is being held to a nigh-impossible standard; all things considered, they must be given credit for what they managed to achieve this year.

Some teams, on the other hand, vastly disappointed this year. Ineos has seemed a bit of a rudderless ship for several seasons now, and they continued to flounder. Carlos Rodriguez was expected to be a GC threat, but despite his seventh place finish he was never really in the running for a podium spot or stage wins. Egan Bernal continues to struggle on the long road back from injury. The team's direction, as a whole, seems questionable. They must determine their identity going forward in the calendar and as the years pass by to reclaim their former glory. Lastly, recently rechristened Red Bull-Bora-Hansgrohe…well. Primož Roglič crashing out would hurt any team, but when your entire goal is to chase the Yellow Jersey and your leader goes out of the race for the third time in his last three Tours de France, it's only going to end up a disappointing year. Jai Hindley managed to salvage a top twenty, but there was little to celebrate for a team expected to compete at the head of the race.

—Young riders: the future is bright

Remco Evenepoel proved that he deserves all the hype. A third place finish in his first ever Tour de France, the White Jersey, a stage win, and proof that he can, for the most part, hang with the world's best climbers in the high mountains? He set himself apart from the field by sticking with Pogačar and Vingegaard day-in and day-out, and it will be exciting to watch his career as a GC threat develop. Matteo Jorgenson and Derek Gee lived up to expectations with top-ten finishes; though neither won a stage, Jorgenson was highly visible day-in and day-out at the head of the race in the mountains and Gee maintained a steady if unassuming presence in the most important moments despite having little support from his team.

Santiago Buitrago managed a tenth place finish, hanging around in all the important days. It was a somewhat disappointing race from Arnaud de Lie considering the hype around him coming into the Tour, but he gets a bit of a pass insofar as this was his debut Grand Tour. Oh, and as a reminder: Tadej Pogačar? Still only twenty-five years old. It's safe to say that cycling will be in good hands for years to come.

—Parting thoughts

Year in and year out we avidly follow a group of 180 men on bikes around France. Through cities, across sprawling fields of sunflowers, up mountain passes, their fates provide a dramatic thread wending its way through the doldrums of summer across the world. Whether meeting with triumph or despair at the end of the three weeks of racing, the cyclists who complete the Tour de France have accomplished something incredible. Be it Tadej Pogačar continuing to author a career that will one day assuredly stand among the greats, Mark Cavendish closing the cover on his own book of records, or a seemingly nameless and faceless *domestique* finishing in the middle of the pack, content with reaching the finale in one piece, it's impossible to overstate what it means to complete a Grand Tour successfully. *Chapeau* to all the riders, congratulations to the winners, and cheers to another Tour de France in the books. *Vive le Tour!*

2024 Tour de France Afterword

The Tour keeps going, a new edition every year. It is our intention to publish a Kindle and audio book every year, to be available in the fall, covering that summer's Tour. This will enable you to keep up with our story as time goes by.

About the Authors

Bill and Carol McGann have had their lives inextricably tied up with bicycles about as long as they can remember. Their first date was a bike ride. Bill, formerly a Category One racer, has been a contributor to several cycling magazines and National Public Radio. He is widely acknowledged as an expert on road bikes and cycling history. Since his father gave him a small one-speed English lightweight bicycle when he was five years old, Bill has been in love with everything about bikes. His wife Carol is a former college biology instructor and is also an accomplished rider, having cycle-toured extensively. Together they started Torelli Imports in 1981, a firm specializing in high-performance cycle equipment. In 2007 they sold the firm. Today, they live in the Oregon's Willamette Valley where they write, manage McGann Publishing and do what they can to keep their cat Andrew happy.

David L. Stanley holds a B.Sc. in zoology, an M.A. in teaching, and is an educator, author, voice-over actor, and speaker. His first book, *Melanoma, It Started with a Freckle*, was released in March, 2016 by McGann Publishing and rapidly became #1 in dermatology and skin wellness. His second book, released in October, 2019, is *From Jim Crow to CEO, the Willie Artis Story*. He worked with Willie Artis, a Black industrialist born in Memphis during the Great Depression who rose to great success in their shared hometown of Flint, MI.

His free-lance work has appeared in national magazines on topics from men, cancer, depression and suicide, fatherhood, and professional bicycle racing. In addition, he co-hosts a podcast titled The Feed Zone which focuses on pro cycling.

The poet-in-residence at TEDx event, Indiana University in 2023, his poetry has appeared in *Aproprose Journal*, *DiVerses*, *Flyover Country*, *The Good Men Project*, *High Summer*, *Porchlight Posts*, *Raven's Perch*, *SamFiftyFour*, *Soundings*, *Stanchion*, *Stand*, and *The State News*.

His sonnets on the Black Lives Matter movement are displayed and archived at the University of Michigan-Flint Library.

Aaron Stanley's lifelong attachment to the world of cycling began before he could walk. His father, David, trained on his rollers with baby Aaron nearby, took him to road criteriums and track races throughout his childhood, and made sure to have the Tour de France broadcast playing in the background every July. Whether it was watching grainy videos of Johan Museeuw winning Paris-Roubaix or anxiously awaiting the Tour preview edition of VeloNews, Aaron grew up with cycling media a part of his life. Nowadays, he works from home in Michigan in the health insurance industry, giving him ample time to pursue his passion for training on the bike, following every ProTour race he can, and spending more than his fair share of time watching, reading, thinking, and writing about sports, cycling chief among them.

Index